Energizing Work and

# CHARGE YOURSELF UP
## FOR SUCCESS

**Doug D. Gordon**

Copyright © 2023 by Doug D. Gordon

Independently published on Amazon

# WHAT OTHERS ARE SAYING

"I have known Doug for a number of years now and we have lunched, met on hikes, shared the stage and been on radio together. Doug mixes his successful corporate experience, where he was a business head for Ireland's biggest stockbroker with his now proven skills in coaching, speaking and training to support everyone from C-level executives to sports stars to film stars.

The content in this book will help you create more success, more energy and more fulfilment within your life and business. I fully recommend this book and Doug Gordon for all he does".

*Eamonn Quinn, Chairman of Kelsius, Chairman of DCU Educational Trust, Chairman of Buymie, former Superquinn (now SuperValu shopping empire).*

"I've had the privilege of being on several panels with Doug and watched him coach. He is a master communicator as well as magnificent mentor! His passion and enthusiasm along with his deep understanding of the human psyche and how to motivate whomever he is speaking to is inspiring. If you're looking to take your life and your career to the next level for whatever goals you are seeking to succeed at, Doug and this book will help you get there. It's an honour to know him."

*Tasia Valenza, Hollywood Actress ( Emmy Award winning Star Wars Actress)*

When I initially met Doug Gordon I was struck with his powerful and welcoming energy. As I got to know him better, I learned this was more a result of intention than accident. In his book, "Charge yourself up for Success" Doug provides the proven processes that can enable all of us to up our game in life and business. Read it and reap!

*Jack Daly; Serial Entrepreneur, CEO Coach, Best Selling Author (UK and Australian speaker of the year)*

"Been on stage with Doug, seen him in action, done radio shows with him. I have to say this is definitely a book worth reading. Between his corporate career where he was in the national press, and now his speaking and coaching career he definitely comes from a place of knowing and inspiration".

*Keith Barry, TV celebrity magician, hypnotist and mentalist*

"In this day of age when high success and high stress seem to go hand in hand, my good friend Doug has mastered the art and broken the code to how to achieve the life you love, the success you deserve without the stress involved. I invite you to read this book and then begin to live the life that you deserve."

*Lisa Nichols, NY Times Bestseller & star of the Secret Book, that has sold over 30 million copies.*

"I have worked with Doug on live and virtual stages and on radio and social media platforms a number of times and we have become friends. He has a unique mix of corporate, entrepreneurial and coaching wisdom and success. His concepts and content is savy. It more than adds value. It energizes efficient action and makes you think more profoundly about what your contribution in life is to the planet. I definitely recommend both Doug and his new book to help you create more wealth, wellbeing and for certain, greater overall fulfillment in life"

*Dr John Demartini – International Bestselling author of The Values Factor and star of the Secret film & book (sold over 30 million copies)*

"Having traveled to the North Pole, South Pole and peaked Everest twice I love hanging around with Inspiring people who are full of positive energy. Doug is definitely one of them and we have become great friends over the years. If you are looking for a way to boost your energy, improve your relationships and be successful in life then this book is a definite read for you. Doug is full of insights, wisdom and inspiration whether on stage, on the screen or on the radio; I highly recommend him as one of the best in the personal and professional development business".

*Pat Falvey Explorer, author, firm producer, mentor, coach.*

"Optimize your energy to optimize your performance in life with Doug's superb new book."

*Stephen M. R. Covey, The New York Times bestselling author of The Speed of Trust and Trust & Inspire*

# ACKNOWLEDGEMENTS

I would like to dedicate this book to my Children Josh and Sarah. I love them with all of my heart and thank them for being my greatest teachers.

I am sincerely grateful to Gosia Wojciulewicz who helped listen to a lot of the book and feed back insights and inspiration.

I am also grateful to my parents and my family for their support.

I am also grateful to all of the kind people who have helped me either with testimonials or promotion of my book. In particular thank you to Lisa Nichols, Eamonn Quinn, Dr John Demartini, Tasia Valenza, Stephen M.R. Covey, Keith Barry, Pat Falvey, and Jack Daly. They are all inspirational people who I have shared the stage with either virtually or in person and having met all of them, they really are as inspiring off stage as they are on.

I also want to thank the Institute of Directors in India for their promotion, Together Magazine, Global Woman Magazine, Positive Life Magazine and all my radio guests. Plus my publisher.

Thank you all for your help in support of this book.

# TABLE OF CONTENTS

| | |
|---|---|
| Preface | 11 |
| Introduction: How to Create Purpose In Life And Business | 14 |
| The Awareness of Managing Your Mind | 31 |
| Reprogramming Your Mindset for Success | 39 |
| The Power Of Letting Go To Be Your Best Self | 48 |
| How To Turn Your Mess into a Message And Give It Meaning | 55 |
| The Millionaire Morning Routine To Energize Your Life | 75 |
| Using Energy for Conscious Creation through a Conscious Mind | 86 |
| Effective Goalsetting And Action Planning In Life & Business | 108 |
| Mindset, Actions, Knowledge, Energy "MAKE" business through Client Mapping | 116 |
| Mastering The Art Of Creating Goals Through Energetic Intention | 143 |
| Success without Stress: Body, Mind And Soul Energy Techniques | 170 |
| The Success Formula To GLEAM Your Energy Out to The World | 182 |
| Appendix: Background Of The Author | 193 |

# PREFACE

Would you like to have more energy in life? Or a life of meaning and purpose? Or to be able to let go of those things that trigger you? Or have better relationships? Or have more fun in life? Or more love in your life? Or be more successful in life? Or achieve your goals faster and easier? Or have less stress in your life? Or even know what the meaning of this thing we call life?

If you answered yes to any of the above questions, this is the book for you.

The book is based around almost 300 interviews with some of the most successful people in the world— and I mean success in life, not necessarily money. New York Times bestselling authors, film stars, TV Celebrities, sports stars, and famous speakers. It is also based around my own experiences in life as a four-time award-winning CEO and coach. It covers all areas of life both outside and inside work.

It will give you a proven success formula, a proven energy enhancement formula, a formula to create more love in your life and ways to improve you emotional intelligence in order to create win-win in life.

Working hard doing something you love never seems stressful, however, when you have to work hard doing the things you don't enjoy, then that isn't fun. This is why it is so important to find out what you love doing or create a sense of love and meaning for what you are already doing.

My main purpose in life and in this book is to inspire people to connect to their true selves, their best selves, in order to find out what their true purpose or mission is in life and go out there and do it. This book will help you find your purpose or create a sense of purpose in what you do.

It will also help you utilize self-awareness to understand your triggers, traits, and programs that you are playing that don't serve you, sabotage you, or are holding you back in life in some way. I will give you a system to reframe the past and let go of those energy-draining character traits and then create new, more positive patterns and habits into your mindset. Awareness is also important in business, in terms of situational awareness (the market, the economy, the product peer group), team awareness (understanding different people have different perspectives, angles and ways of seeing things), organizational awareness (understanding that there are different departments/teams or groups within organizations that have different tasks and different agendas and it is important to respect, collaborate and work together in harmony) and client awareness (understanding the client's expectations and needs) all which come from having good knowledge of the people around you, the market, the economy and the character types you are interacting with.

This book will help you to understand how you can optimize your energy to optimize your life; enabling you to get more done in less time with less stress and to improve your relationships with yourself and others to create WIN-WIN in life.

We talk mindset, actions, and knowledge from some of the top minds in the world and give tips on how to optimize your relationships, your work, and your entire life.

The book then goes onto how you can create your best life and how to align your goals to your purpose in order to create direction in your life or for the lives of the people in your business or your personal life.

We will talk conscious communication skills, how to be a conscious leader, a conscious parent, a better lover, and how to create more wealth, better health, and more happiness in your life.

Enjoy the journey!

INTRODUCTION

# HOW TO CREATE PURPOSE IN LIFE AND BUSINESS

Have you ever struggled to get out of bed in the morning? You may have had eight hours of great sleep and yet when the alarm goes off, you may have pressed that snooze button again and again, until eventually, you sat up on the side of the bed and said, "Oh crap! Not again! Why do I do this every flipping day? This is like groundhog day. God, please help me?" Then, you dragged yourself to the bathroom, still half-asleep, almost tripping over the bathroom mat and into the bath on the way, dragged yourself out the door, dragged yourself into the office, and then sat there staring at a screen all day, wondering what on the earth are you are doing there! Yet, another day when you were going on holiday, and you may have only had three hours sleep because you were up late packing, this time, the alarm goes off and you spring out of bed, spring into a taxi, spring into the airplane, and then spring into the swimming pool in the hotel at your destination with loads of energy. Why? Because you are aligned with something you love doing. When you are aligned with a sense of LOVE for what you are doing you have LOTS OF VIBRANT ENERGY, and if you optimize your energy, you can optimize your life and your work.

Energy produces vitality, helps you focus better, perform better, be more productive, have better relationships, and get more done in less time with less stress. People talk about how important time management is, but actually energy management is so much more important. If you are in the energetic zone of pure focus, you will optimize your time so much more. When you are in your highest state of energy, you tend to be your best self. You can deal with the stresses and strains of life more easily. With more energy, you will even be better in bed with your partner, as, one, you will be gleaming with positive energy, radiating love, and two, you will have a little bit extra power in the engine, if you know what I mean… vroom, vroom!!! You will have more endurance, more control, more vibrancy, and more enthusiasm for the job; every bed partner's dream.

If you think about it, everything in life is energy. Thoughts are energy, words or speech are energy. Thoughts lead to words, words lead to actions, actions lead to habits, and habits lead to destiny. So, start with a positive thought, and you will end with a positive destiny.

The question is where do you start? What is the definition in terms of success in life? Success is different for everyone, and it is defined by you and what you want to achieve. It is so important to make sure that your life is designed around your personal goals that are aligned to you and you alone. Too many people focus and compare themselves to other people—maybe a father, mother, brother, or sister, and they want to be like them and follow their dreams and their goals, rather than what's truly in their own heart. That is why is it so important to find out what you love doing the most and then follow your dream. So, my question for you is: what do you love doing? What do you talk about the most? What activity do you find yourself springing out of bed for in the morning? What are you naturally good at doing? If you can look at all those questions and decipher an answer and see if you can add value to people in some way or form so that you can make money out of it, then hey, presto, you are a path of purpose.

I remember when I was eight years old, my Uncle Stuart said to me, "Doug, what would you like to be when you are older?"

I told him, "I want to be a brain surgeon". He laughed and asked me, "Why"?

"Because I love chatting with people and helping them." He laughed even louder at me, almost falling off his chair in the process, reminding me that a surgeon wouldn't be able to talk to people while doing the surgery.

It's funny how now I am working with people helping them implement neuro-plastic change within their brain in terms of reframing past traumas and experiences in order to create new patterns in the way they think, speak, and act, so that they are happier, healthier, and wealthier in terms of the richness of life. Or I am helping them dream bigger, plan better, organize more efficiently, so that their business grows at a faster pace. Or I am helping them see their relationships in a different perspective, helping them to have more positive emotionally intelligent relationships with their loved ones or colleagues.

Success truly is all about connecting with your true self, your inner heart self, and then understanding what your true mission or purpose is in life. Once you know what this is, then having clear, defined goals that lead you on an inspiring journey through life that gives you a sense of satisfaction and love within your heart along the way, is one of the true definitions of success. Remember though, it's not just about the end results—it is about the enjoyment of the journey along the way. The learnings of life, the people you meet, the places you go, the experiences you have will mold you into the character that you become and that can be a lot of fun!

As I said, be careful not to get wrapped up in someone else's dream, someone else's purpose, unless it truly aligns to you and your heart. Quite often, our parents push us down a route that isn't necessarily our true path, or we have a father or mother who was so busy working when we were younger we didn't get the attention or love that we needed, and then, when we grow up, we model their path to try and get their attention and their love. This was my initial path; my dad was my super hero, but he was a busy man, and on the weekends when I was young, he spent a lot of time playing sports and socializing with his friends and then was too tired to give his best self for the remainder of the weekend. He was very hard-working and stressed, and I certainly have no blame, but it did make me seek his approval all the time. This was then replicated with a number of my bosses in my early part of my career. He was in the financial world, so I went into the same thing. He played hockey, so I did, too. Many of us often do this; as young adults, we try and emulate our parents, so that they like us more because we are still seeking that love and attention that we felt we didn't get as a young child. The only problem is we sometimes make our life goals all about ego and trying to impress our parents, rather than actually following our heart and true purpose.

I don't know about you, but when I was coming out of university, I had clearly defined goals in my mind. Most of them were aligned to ego, competition, and impressing my father. Regardless, they were clear in my mind, and through my competitive nature, I was determined to achieve them. I wanted to be a six-figure earner within five years, which I told a few housemates, and they laughed, thinking it would never happen, as we were studying engineering, which didn't pay well in the U.K. I wanted to be recognized for being successful in my industry and become a millionaire. I wanted a house and a holiday home like my father paid off with no mortgage, and I wanted a family with a couple of kids. I also wanted to have a lot of fun along the way and not have to work that hard to get there. Within five years, I was earning over a hundred thousand sterling a year in the investment management world. By the time I was 35, I had a four-bedroom house with no mortgage, and I'd bought a holiday home for cash. I was married and had two lovely kids, Josh and Sarah. I also had another goal that my kids would be two-and-a-half years apart, so that Josh, the oldest, would be walking and out of nappies before Sarah was born. Sarah was born exactly two-and-a-half years after Josh, to the day. I also was a millionaire based on real estate, cash, and my investments. Looking in from the outside, you would think I had the perfect life, even ski holidays every year, sun holidays, five-star hotels, Michelin-star restaurants, and many glamorous events and parties. The problem was inside, I wasn't happy, and the reason being was the money, the goals, the lifestyle was all ego, and I was not aligned to a sense of higher purpose. Or I hadn't created the understanding of how the energetics of what I did added value to human lives, giving it meaning and purpose.

In 2014, my father-in-law at the time had been diagnosed with kidney failure and bone cancer, and considering he was eighty, we were told he wouldn't have long to live. In 2015, I left a high-profile job in London with Columbia Threadneedle Investments as Sales Director and took the family back to Ireland, where my father-in-law lived, with the goal of his daughter and grandchildren being there for him in his last years to make him happy. I figured if I was in his shoes, I would have loved that, so it was the best gift I could give him. He lived up until summer 2021, showing that happiness and company of loved ones is one of the most powerful reasons to help someone have a sense of purpose. I noticed that his health deteriorated when the children got older and there was less dependency on needing his help. It was lovely, though, as both kids spoke beautifully with true love about their grandfather at his funeral. They had the privilege of getting to know this great man in his final years, and they loved him with all of their hearts. I loved him, too, and admired him, because although he wasn't the richest of men in the world, he had a happy life. He traveled the world, he ran marathons, he cycled from one end of Scotland to the other end of England, he built eighty-year friendships, he had two wonderful children, five beautiful grandchildren, and he spent time getting to know each one with great interest. Perhaps he wasn't rich in money, but he was rich in life.

When I moved back to Dublin, there was an article in the national newspapers saying that I was joining Davy, Ireland's leading stockbroker, and the title of the article was "Davy Appoints City Heavy Hitter Doug Gordon." This was a humbling recognition of success in my industry, and another goal achieved, albeit coming from a bit of ego. The article was written as I had been selling funds to large institutions in Dublin as well as London and between two large Italian fund managers and Davy, themselves, I had brought in almost one billion euros of business from my Dublin accounts. The Dublin investment industry is so small that everyone knows everyone. You literally can't say boo without someone hearing about it, so this information had been well-sourced before I was hired. I had also grown the client assets that I was responsible for in Columbia Threadneedle, from $50 million per annum sales to $1.75 billion per annum sales in six years. Thankfully, the year I did the $1.75 billion, it was very easy to see the proof, as one deal was written about in the trade press for £285 million and another was from a fund manager with public factsheets, so you could see at the start of the year how many assets they had with Columbia Threadneedle and at the end of the year too. They added over £550 million and what was amazing about this second client was at the start of the year, there was a threat of losing £285 million of investment they had in one of our funds. The reason for this threat was we had an entire fund management team leave the company where they held those assets. That's like a racing car team losing their star drivers; it makes it a hard bet to continue following.

The reason for telling you this isn't to showcase how great my achievements are; it is to showcase that I had very clear, defined goals in my head that I energetically thought about all the time and being in that thought energy helped me achieve them. The goals also helped others benefit from them, too. Becoming a millionaire enabled my family and kids to be well looked after. The recognition of success benefited my company I worked for and the clients who bought the products that I sold, as they were in great-performing products, and I believed in them. Also, by bringing a lot of revenue into the business, the money was used to pay for more staff, which in turn benefited their families and more people.

Another university goal of mine was to be successful in sport, and I used to play top level field hockey all the way up until I was forty (at one stage captaining and coaching internationals at first team level, in fact, in university, I played in the same team as Jason Lee, who was one of the top center forwards in the U.K. and went on to coach the Great Britain team in the 2012 Olympics). In my corporate career, I often left work at 5:30 p.m. on the dot to get home for training. One day, the CEO of one company asked me, "What is the secret to your success, Doug? You seem to do the least amount of hours in the sales team and get the most amount of business in— I don't get it." I said to him, "Positive mindset. Lots of focused activity in terms of calls and meetings. Knowledge of the clients and their needs. Plus, lots of vibrant energy." This is where I came up with my success formula using the acronym of MAKE; standing for Mindset or Motivation, Action or Activities, Knowledge or Knowing State, and Energy. I love to play on words and use words in a fun way, in this case, it referred to MAKE more sales. However, it can refer to MAKE the best you, MAKE the best relationship, MAKE a business successful, MAKE yourself into perfect health. You can pretty much use the acronym for success in anything.

In terms of mindset, it is so important to motivate yourself to be the best version of yourself every day and then help motivate the other people around you in life and in business to do the same as well. If, in business, for example, it is important to motivate your clients to buy your products or services, and in terms of actions or activities, it is all about understanding where you are in life or your business and where you want to go. That can come down to setting clearly defined goals and having a clear vision of the outcomes you want, then putting a plan in place to get there. Knowledge in terms of business is about knowing your product, knowing your client, knowing your industry, and matching your client needs to your USPs (unique selling points). Or having a knowing faith or state in terms of your mind and vision. You might ask me what I mean by that— well, if you asked me my name, I would obviously say Doug. The question, then, is, "Do I think my name is Doug, do I believe my name is Doug, or do I just know my name is Doug?" I know it, of course. So know what you truly want in life and have absolute faith that regardless of the ups and downs, you are going to achieve it. The final part is energy. In all my time in business, it was not necessarily the employees with PhDs or MBAs who were the most successful, it was the people with the greatest amount of positive energy who got up every day with a true drive and zest to succeed, regardless of what happened along the way.

Positive people, who take positive actions, produce positive results most of the time, and this is why having a positive mind is so important. People talk about getting into a positive flow state, or if in sport, getting into the zone, in order to perform to your very best. I have been in this zone state while playing field hockey, where I literally have glided past two players with ease and smacked the ball into the top of the net without even thinking about it. Even writing this book, there were nights where I worked until 5:30 a.m. because I was in that focused state where the words just seemed to effortlessly come out. This flow state is where awareness and action merge to create a pure state of absolute focus. The flow state has been studied closely by the researchers at McKinsey and Company, where they did a ten-year study on flow and productivity and showed that employees in the flow are on average 500 percent more productive than those who were not. This is where their energy was optimized, their focus was perfect, and they were at an optimal state in terms of productivity. Everything just flowed for them and the people around them.

There was even a Forbes magazine article showing that happier staff are 20 percent more productive, and happier sales people are 37 percent more productive. In fact, there was another article in Fortune magazine showing the stock market prices of the "100 Best Companies to Work for" rose 14 percent per annum from 1998 to 2005, while companies not on the list only reported only a six percent increase on average. When I read this, being an ex-stock market guy, I did some research myself and found that the stock market goes up 80 percent of the time the day before Easter, the day before Independence Day, the day before Thanksgiving, and the last two weeks of the year, during what they call the Santa rally. Why? Because people are happy that they are going to have a holiday the next day or are already on holiday at the end of the year. They are happy they are going to be with their family and friends or doing something they love. So, as I said, positive people produce positive results and outcomes. That positivity and happiness factor affects not only people, but also the entire global economic system, and that is why it is so important to get yourself, your family, and your employees, if in a business, into the happiest state possible. It even affects your health; have you ever noticed that the happier people tend to stay healthier?

The question is how can we get ourselves or our employees to spring into the office or into action with the same sense of love and positivity every single day?

When I was working in the investment world selling hedge and mutual funds to financial institutions, I didn't always spring out of bed. Having said that, I loved the people aspect of the job, I loved the challenge of putting a large deal together, I loved finding out what their needs were in respect to their client portfolios and seeing if we had a fund that could fit those needs to add value. I enjoyed my job, and that was why I was able to grow an asset management business from $50 million per annum sales to $1.75 billion per annum sales in six years. Like many people though, I was largely motivated by money and when I first started in the industry, we used to get paid quarterly sales bonuses, and there would always be a sense of excitement when it came around to the end of the quarter. That excitement bred positivity, and quite often, the sales guys would land a few extra deals at the end of the quarter because they were in a positive mood and that reflected in the way they worked. Interestingly, as time went on, the industry moved more towards yearly bonuses, mainly because anyone outside of the sales team wouldn't be getting a quarterly one, so they wanted to keep the entire organization aligned to the same process. Good for anyone outside of sales, but not so good for the sales people, and at the end of the day, the more sales that come in, the more profits, and the more profits, the bigger the bonuses for everyone, thus making everyone happier. The problem was; some people's egos got in the way, and other people just wanted easier administration of only having to do one bonus run for everyone at the same time. It might save money for the human resource department, but in terms of the happiness of the sales team and the overall profitability of the business based on the statistics I showed earlier; which do you think is better?

Happiness isn't all about money, though. It is about being aligned to that true sense of purpose, and purpose can create a more positive atmosphere both within your psyche and within your business. A recent simple study shown on the Web used a fun digital exercise where they asked people to play a computer game where they had to take a small circular object from the top of the screen and put it into a square object on the other side of the screen. It was tested with three sets of people. To the first set of people, they offered them $5 to do it as much as possible. The second set, they offered 50 cents. The third set, they didn't offer them any money, but instead, they told them it was for a cause to do with mental health and to help people in terms of a charity.

The first set of people, paid $5, averaged about 151 times of completing the task. The people paid 50 cents averaged about a hundred times. This shows that there was a direct correlation to how much they were paid and the number of times that they completed the task. What is amazing is the third set, the people who weren't paid anything but because they were doing it for a cause or a charity, the average increased to 162 times. This shows the positive effect of creating a sense of purpose for you and your business. It may be that you give a percentage of your earnings to a worthy charity, one that is meaningful to you. Or through designing an effective mission statement or purpose for your business, and what you do, you can considerably increase your or your team's performance.

On this point, I had a personal experience with an IT guy who worked for me at one company— let's call him Chris— who came up to me one day and said, "Doug, I am fed up, all I do all day is fix IT problems, and all I get is people complaining about the computer systems being down and the IT not working. I am fed up I want to leave."

I said to him, "Chris, reframe it in a different way. What is it we do as a company?"

Chris replied, "We are an investment company providing investments and pensions for people."

I replied, "Yes, but what we are actually doing is aiming to outperform the stock market and other pension plans, in order to give that granny or grandpa a better retirement plan, so that they can buy a better retirement home, go on better holidays, give more to their children, or give more to their grandchildren. Basically, we are making their lives better. So every time you solve one of those IT issues, you are enabling us to do better online research, better deals, better valuations, and produce better results for that granny or grandpa. In other words, every single time you solve an IT issue, you are helping make someone's life better."

Once I had helped Chris reframe his thoughts, he felt a sense of meaning and purpose in what he was doing because he realized that his actions were aligned to helping a real person's life be bettered in a positive way.

This idea can be applied to a secretary, a janitor, or even the CEO—it doesn't matter, the importance is to instill the understanding of how everyone's actions and energy they put in can impact the end granny or grandpa, mother or father, brother or sister, son or daughter in some way or form.

This comes from conscious communication from management engaging with staff, so they have a clear understanding of what the company is doing, why they are doing it, and reminding their staff on a regular basis. The mission statement of the company needs to cover this, but the problem is most mission statements come from a place to impress, rather than to bless, and the only time the staff are reminded of the mission statement or purpose is when they join the company and at the annual conference. Mission statements and sense of purpose needs to be made fun, come from the heart, and be instilled into the hearts of every employee in the company, so that they have a true sense of love for what they do, love for the product or service they provide, love for the people they work with, and love for the clients they serve. As said before, LOVE is an acronym for LOTS OF VIBRANT ENERGY – which is what you want in your organization and in your own personal life.

On a much grander scale, this can be highlighted in the true story of when Nelson Mandela became president of South Africa in 1994. There were big problems in terms of conflicts between Black and white societies within South Africa and Nelson Mandela, who was Black, himself, wanted to bring the country together as one united nation. Remember, this was a guy who had spent 27 years in a prison, suddenly wanting to create unity in a very divided country. He was a man on a mission, and he had a massive sense of purpose in what he was doing. The question was how could he do it in a positive way?

In 1994, he attended a rugby match where South Africa played England. England won easily 32 points to 15. South Africa, at the time, was a top tier rugby nation, but of the top tier, they were considered second rate, and most felt they didn't have a hope in winning the 1995 Rugby World Cup, which they were hosting in South Africa. During the England match, Nelson Mandela saw the South African whites cheering on South Africa, but the Blacks cheering on England. Rugby was seen as a white sport, and they were not prepared to support their oppressors. Nelson Mandela saw an opportunity; he saw the passion in the crowds of the sport, and he found out that over a billion people would be watching the World Cup on television. He wanted to utilize the support for the nation's rugby team to unite the people as one, giving them a common mission, goal, and a sense of purpose. He met with François Pienaar, the South African captain, and asked him if he would work with him in terms of using rugby to unite the country and see if they could win the World Cup. François studied Mandela and was inspired by his passion. He took that energy and inspired the rest of the team with the same inspiration he had gained from Nelson Mandela. The team trained harder than they ever had before, and even in their busy training schedule, they went around to all the Black communities, playing and teaching rugby to the kids across the country. They created a positive energy around the sport with the Black communities and created a positive bond between the predominately a white rugby team and the Black communities as well. It was a genius move by Mandela. What it also did, though, was give the South African rugby team a true sense of purpose in terms of winning the World Cup. The energy behind their purpose was not about the ego of competition nor the ego of being the winner—it was about bringing the whole nation together as one to create a sense of community and positive connection or even love. They got all the way to the final against New Zealand, who were a phenomenal team, and no one expected South Africa to win. In fact, the bookies and betting agents had bets that South

Africa were going to easily lose. François Pienaar and his team played the game of their lives. They played with a true sense of love for their country, and South Africa won by 15 to 12 points. The nation erupted in celebration, and there were Blacks and whites hugging and dancing together on the streets. The nation had been brought together through rugby. It really showed how sport can be an amazing way of bringing different communities together on the national level. This story of inspiration from Nelson Mandela is told beautifully in the film Invictus, which I highly recommend. Emulating these kind of tactics in business as well can be very beneficial for a company or organization.

So how else do we create more of this love and positivity within businesses or even our own families? Well, I was in Monte Carlo a few years ago staying in the Hermitage Hotel, which is a superb hotel with immaculate service and staff, in case you are ever heading that way. Every day, I would see the concierge full of positive energy, always happy and helpful. After two days, I went up to him and said, "Philippe, you have such amazing energy, and I love the way you are always so helpful with everyone. What is your secret?"

Philippe replied, "Ah, Mr. Gordon, it is my manager. He is one of the nicest fellows I have ever worked with. Every day, he asks me if there is anything he can do to help me, is there anything he can do to make my job easier, or is there anything he can do to make my life better, and he really means it! I feel appreciated and loved. So, all I have to give out to our customers is love and appreciation. In my last job in another hotel, my boss watched me all the time, making sure I was doing my job correctly, looking after the customers in the right way. I always felt like I was being watched, and I was fearful of making a mistake, and this came across to the customers, and in turn, I wasn't as good at my job."

Philippe's point was so important; managers need to be showing appreciation, gratitude, trust, and love for their staff because if you look after your staff, they will look after the customers for you. A person full of love can only give out love. A person who is fearful is not as effective, so give love to your staff and watch the magic that happens. This is the same in parenting and relationships.

A lot of what I have said is based around working for a company or an organization and creating purpose based on what you are already doing. I often get asked, what if you are just starting off, or you don't know what you are meant to be doing in life, or you are not sure of your purpose? Well, a good start is to write down five things you love doing, five things you are good at doing, and five things that you can do to add value to people in some way or form. Then, see if there is a match between all those three questions, and then, go out and do it. You will never work a day, as you will be doing something you love and something in service to others, so it will give you a sense of fulfillment within. Another way of deciding what your path or purpose in life is to imagine if I gave you a speaking slot at one of my events where you would be ninety years of age, delivering your legacy speech to an audience of 100,000 people live and a billion people on television all around the world at the same time. What would you love to talk about most? What could you say to add the most value and impact for the audience in the most positive way? Imagine it was the last thing you would ever leave in terms of communication on this planet. Then, once you know your subject, reverse engineer yourself back to where you are today. What action steps, research, education, and jobs do you need to do today to lead you towards being truly worthy to step up in front of those 100,000 people? This way, you will have a good idea of where to start and what you can be doing in the present moment to create the future you want.

These steps are designed to help you find a sense of purpose in life or create one in the existing business you are in. Having purpose brings more passion, more energy, and more focus. Overall, it is a massive step towards high performance success without stress because you will never mind working hard for something that you love doing.

In terms of purpose, you might ask yourself, "what is the purpose of life?" Well, in my opinion, life is about becoming your true, authentic best self and connecting with that true self through your heart and soul. Then, making all decisions in life from that connection, with a sense of gratitude, love and authenticity. On top of that, connect to what aligns with your heart in terms of your true purpose and mission in life. I also believe in a spiritual context that we come down as humans to experience life in physicality, learning from these experiences in order to grow and evolve as a soul and then teach others what we learn, so that they can go through the experiences in a more conscious manner. One of my theories is the idea of reincarnation, so that we can come down as male, female, sportsman, businessman, doctor, actor, king, queen, beggar, billionaire, all different roles in different lives, all different people to experience different perspectives in this game of life, so that we can understand from different angles how life can be. Perhaps, for example, the German leader Adolf Hitler may have come down as a victim in his next life, playing the role in reverse of what he caused in terms of the Jews during World War II. A sense of karma in terms of what you give out you get back, what you do unto others will come back to you. I also believe that souls can come down here for a lifetime or sometimes for a very short period of time to help and support others with their missions too. For example, I had a friend called Gary in the investment world who was a lovely guy, but unfortunately, he had a devastating experience where he lost his child to cot death only three months after the child was born. My friend became an inspiration, helping charities and other children based around the experience he had. His child, in the short space of time on this planet, changed Gary in such a positive way that he then impacted hundreds and thousands of lives all over the world. The ripple effect of his child's death and the charity that he did afterwards to help others was truly inspirational. Some people can have a mission in life to help millions of people and others just help and change one person's life. That one person, though, can go on to help more people, and the ripple effect leads to indirectly helping millions of people. So, the next time you think there were only a few people that you helped in a situation where you wanted to help hundreds, maybe just one of those people went on to help the hundreds for you, based on what you said or did for them. Remember it only takes one seed to grow an apple tree, and from that one apple tree, fruit can fall with seeds in them that can grow other trees, and the ripple effect can grow an entire orchard over time. All starting with just one single seed. So, as you can see from what my friend Gary went through, sometimes you can create purpose in your life by turning your "mess into a message and give it meaning" in some way or form. Learning from a trauma or a tragedy and turning it into a triumph for someone else in the future.

# THE AWARNESS OF MANAGING YOUR MIND

One of my passions in life was to play field hockey. My father played it, as well as my uncle who used to captain Ireland and Great Britain back in the 1960s. He was one of the best strikers ever in the game. I loved it, and every week, I used to look forward to the matches we would play at the weekend. When I was in my late teens, I played in one of the highest leagues for one of the best teams in Europe. If it was soccer, it would be like playing for Manchester United, Real Madrid, or Barcelona. Now, although I had that real sense of purpose when I played and I loved it, I still needed to look at myself and have awareness every day, making sure I was in the best possible state physically, mentally, and emotionally, in order to perform at the highest level. I was playing in a team full of international sportsmen, and there was no room for character flaws or weak-minded emotions. Emotional Intelligence was key to success in the game, and the components of this include self-awareness, self-regulation, empathy, self / team motivation, and social skills in terms of communication and teamwork. Optimizing all of these key components of emotional intelligence is paramount for success, and this is the same in life and in business, as well as sport. Sometimes, we can have traits, trigger points, and habits that hold us back in life, and having self-awareness of these traits is so important. These can be programs or character traits that may have been picked up in childhood, and we need to look at them in a state of awareness, in order to know what they are, so that we can work to change and become a better version of ourselves. Once we know what these flaws are, we can reprogram ourselves through auto-suggestion, new habit-forming, and neuroplasticity. Neuroplasticity is where new neural pathways, patterns, or memories are formed within the brain and in turn, create new character habits and new patterns within your psyche. This can be really important in life in terms of your relationships in love, in work, and in families, as these past trigger points can cause blow-ups in certain situations, which will not serve you in any way. By working on them through self-awareness, you can stop doing them, then you can plant new seeds or ideas in your head again and again, in order to create a new habit so that leads you to deal with the situation better when triggered in the future or to enable you not to be triggered at all.

Let's face it: sometimes, when going into a relationship or employing a new staff member, you don't know all of the past experiences the person has had or the baggage they may be carrying inside of them that might trigger them in some way or form. If you are a corporation or business, you can use my behavioral awareness exercises in the next chapter to help your employees recognize patterns that don't serve them, in order to be able to self-improve and become more emotionally intelligent. This will lead to the future interactions they have, hopefully creating win-win, rather than win-lose with other people. It can be a massively beneficial exercise to create better team environments, better leaders, and better client experiences. Let's face it: there is so much energy wasted in organizations where employees have blow-ups, get overly stressed, hold grudges, or have jealousy towards other colleagues. This can cause a massive amount of wasted time through confrontations and toxic communication between people.

The exercises can also help you have more fulfilling relationships in life yourself, making you a better husband, wife, boyfriend, girlfriend, brother, sister, mother, father or even friend.

I'm sure you have a few traits you know that you have that don't serve you? Right? Go on, admit it: nobody is perfect. So, how can we be the best versions of ourselves when we are carrying around emotional baggage and triggers within us that could blow up at any time? Having these annoying traits can make a person focus too much on the distractions of life, too much on the negatives, and in turn, you may focus on what you don't want, rather than what you do truly want. Plus, as I have already said; where focus goes, energy flows, and you want to focus all your energy on your positive future, not your negative past. Two of the most important commodities in life are time and energy. What differentiates successful people is how they use these two. In order to optimize our energy and create the best possible mindset, sometimes, we need to clean out the old beliefs and subconscious patterns that don't serve us to make room for the new— in other words, empty your cup in order to refill it with fresh ideas.

One of the most important traits of emotional intelligence is empathy and being able to put yourself in the other person's shoes, in order to understand how they see things from their angle and perspective. It is key in all relationships. Let's face it: every one of us is a product of our parents, our preachers, our teachers, our peer groups, and our past relationships. The experiences we have mold us into the people that we are today, and we all have different perspectives and all look at situations and people in different ways. We also communicate from those different viewpoints and that is why it is so important to ask questions to understand others rather than make assumptions. This is normal, this is part of our psyche, this is part of our mindset, this is part of life. You can have one person see a color as yellow and another see it as orange. Neither may be right or neither wrong; it is just two different perspectives of the same thing. If we, as humans, could all respect each other for the fact; that we are 'all' going to have these different realities, different perspectives, and different opinions, then the world would be such a better place; in terms of international, business, and even love relationships. The problem is, everyone has an opinion, and opinions can be like backsides: we all have one, we just don't necessarily want to hear the loud, stinky ones! Wars in the past were started because of difference of opinions, differing viewpoints, and trying to push those on other people and other societies without any respect for them in the first place. This includes wars between people within companies. If people could just respect each other for their different ways of seeing things in life and focus on win-win for you and the other person, rather than win-lose, we would create so much more positivity in the world, in our businesses, and in our relationships. Asking the right questions and seeking to understand the other person's perspective is key to better relationships and better communication; to create better outcomes.

As said before, where focus goes, energy flows, so if you focus on different opinions and negatively complain about them, then you are wasting the energy that you could be using for more positive things in life, like your dreams, your wishes, and your goals. Plus, complaining is the opposite of gratitude, it's low vibration energy and a waste of time. I have sat at dinner tables in the past where people would gossip and complain about other people who weren't even there. They do it for their own entertainment and ego, to make themselves feel better about themselves, by putting other people down, which actually doesn't energetically work. What they are really doing is expressing a deep-set insecurity and a sense of not feeling good enough. Then, in order to outwardly hide that, they put other people down because they think it will make them feel better. What a waste of time and energy because when we negatively put others down, we are actually lowering our own vibrational energy. When we boost people up and talk positively about people, we actually heighten our vibration and heighten our energy. Try it – try talking negatively about someone for a while, and then, in a state of awareness, go inside and see how you feel. Then, do the opposite; really talk with love and kindness about someone, and you will see you get an increase in energy within your body. A much more beneficial use of time and energy in any gathering is to mastermind how you can help other people who might be struggling in order to create positivity for them and their lives. Or masterminding about world peace, a new invention, forming a collective religion of love, helping the needy, or just creating more wealth, health, and happiness in your life or business. That is one of the great advantages of having a diverse and inclusive environment in organizations and within your friendships. The differing backgrounds can give a wider range of viewpoints and perspectives on solving a problem, thus bringing out a wider range of solutions in a speedier fashion. They say that people who have lived and befriended more people from different countries and cultures tend to be more creative in their thinking. This is why I think all companies should work on their diversity and inclusion programs.

We all have worries and problems to consider at certain times, but it is so important to always focus on what you want in the future, rather than what you don't want in your life, so that you are happier, healthier, and more successful. In fact, when you are in the energy of a problem, talking about the past all the time and what someone did to you, or your team, if in business, or your people, if it is a cultural issue, it is much harder to move towards the solution. Yes, it is very important to have compassion, empathy, and understanding for the past wrongs, but then take what you need in terms of the learnings and move out of the energy of the problem towards the energy of the solution as quickly as possible. What can you or we do positively in the now i.e. the present moment, in order to ensure a brighter future for all involved?

On a personal level, the problem often is we tend to have these programs or character traits we are playing which don't serve us, that we have picked up from the past. Most of the time, we learned them from our parents as children. These kinds of programs include traits like; lack of self-love, not actively listening, fear, egotism, defensiveness, being overly competitive, abandonment issues, being controlling, being unauthentic, insecurity, perfectionism, overthinking, being over-emotional, lack of emotional intelligence, and lack of forgiveness, just to name a few.

Parental programs such as worry can cause a massive amount of stress and waste so much thinking time. As I said earlier, thoughts are energy, so don't waste them on negativity; it will drain you. I remember I had a testing boss who was jealous of my success and jealous of me being praised by his boss, the CEO. He loved to put me down in the past, and I would spend entire weekends worrying about what he said to me the previous week and what he might say to me the following week. It was an absolute waste of time and energy. It affected me, and in turn, it affected my closest relationship at the time, my marriage. Even though I kept a lot of the worries to myself, the energy vibration would have felt like a bad smell, and that is not pleasant to live with, for anybody. These negative thoughts can prevent people from focusing on their goals and dreams and cause not just distraction but also stress. In fact, holding onto traits like resentment, anger, lack of forgiveness, or guilt can cause dis-harmony within the body and in turn, cause dis-ease or disease. So, it's pretty important to lose these traits rapidly, so that you can be in the best possible energetic state and be laser-focused on what you want to achieve in life or business, without any negative vibration residing inside of you. This is true in life and in business as well. It is so important in a business or in a family to help and support everyone to come to a state of awareness and acceptance of the traits that don't serve them in a kind, empathetic way, so that people can then positively make changes, to better themselves.

On a personal relationship perspective and something fun that links into the below exercise as well, is a question I had from one of my university friends who is a bit of a joker. He said to me, "So, if I read your book, would it help me to learn how to 'make' my wife have better orgasms?" Now joking aside, let's just think about that for a moment. In my experience, through helping couples, one of the factors that can influence whether or not a woman has an orgasm is her

Mindset. If she is holding on to negative emotions that have either come from a childhood experience, maybe with an absent father. Or a bad past relationship experience. Or maybe even holding onto a grudge in her current relationship. Then these are not going to help. So, in terms of energy blocks and mindset, if she was able to release these suppressed emotions, she might relax more, get into the flow of things, and who knows? In terms of actions, as her husband, he would need to be loving, kind, considerate, supportive, romantic, and woo her in a way that gets her into the right mood. Moving onto knowledge, he would need to learn all about his wife, her interests, what she likes and how he can stimulate her mind first rather than her private parts. He would also need to have good knowledge of her anatomy and what she enjoys and what makes her excited or turned on. Then, finally, in terms of energy, he would need to show her true love, as love is the highest form of energy frequency in existence, and through love and energy connection, you stand a very good chance of achieving your goal. I'm not saying this will universally work, but it may be worth a try! Emotions are energy in motion, and they are meant to flow in and out as we experience life, like the way the water flows along a river. Sometimes, though, the water in a river can get stuck behind a rock at the side of the riverbank, and that water can become murky and even stagnant. This can be like stuck emotions—if you can release them, it can help the energetic flow within you. Emotions are feelings, and feelings are interlinked to behavioral habits and thoughts. Having had 15 years of marriage followed by a lot of experience in dating, my biggest tip for men is to entice a woman through her mind, showing her love and respect. Men are different. In general, ladies, they are much simpler creatures; you can go straight for the crotch, and most will be delighted. Only joking… well kind of!

The good news is I have a mindset reprogramming technique that can help create awareness of these parental programs and stuck emotions. Then through this awareness and acceptance you can implement positive change. The next chapter covers this exercise.

# REPROGRAMMING YOUR MINDSET FOR SUCCESS

Firstly, take a piece of paper and write down all the triggers, traits, flaws, and programs you know and are aware of that you are playing. Be truly honest with yourself. Even if something is only slightly in you, write it down. In the past, mine included being egotistical, opinionated, stubborn, easily distracted by shiny objects, abandonment issues, and lack of self-love. Thankfully though, through conscious awareness and using the exercise in this section, I have worked on all of them and realized that they did not serve me. Quite often, in relationships, someone can feel the need to be right all the time. Maybe next time, consider: "I can be right, or I can be happy". I am sure you would agree it is better to be happy. Next time, just say, "Yes, dear," and let it go. Or really try and ask all the right questions to understand the other person's perspective before pushing your own views across.

Secondly, on a separate piece of paper, list five people in your life that test you or annoy you in some way or form. It could be a mother, a father, a brother, a sister, a son, a daughter, a love partner, or even a boss. I would definitely suggest one of the five to be a mother or father, as we tend to model them in our early years of life. For the first two years we generally can't speak so the programming is all one way. How many times have you caught yourself saying something or doing something and then said to yourself, "Oh no, I'm turning into my mother or father!" Once you have decided on the five people; write down their names, and then, under their names, write down the traits, flaws, or programs that you can see in them that you don't like or do not serve them. Then, look at all those traits of the five people, and see if there is any commonality of those traits between the people you have chosen. If there is a common trait even between two of them; then own it yourself, as it is probably in you as well, even if you don't think so. I believe that people come into our lives for a reason, and quite often they mirror back the areas we need to self-improve on. Sometimes, it can only be slightly in you, but it is still in you. So, own it, and write these mirrored traits down on the other piece of paper where you wrote your own self-aware flaws, adding to the master list.

It is actually a blessing to have a conscious awareness of this mirroring effect because the next time you are ever in an argument with a client, a friend, or a loved one, stop and ask yourself, "What is mirroring back in this interaction? What can I learn from this interaction? And how can I grow to become a better version of myself and create win-win in my future interactions?" It is a powerful way to reframe each interaction in life, take positive responsibility, and see the experience as a learning opportunity, thus creating peace, rather than conflict very quickly. It is also a great way of gamifying life and seeing life as an opportunity to self-improve every day.

In my relationship coaching, I often hear a client tell me that their ex-partner was a narcissist, and I truly believe that this word can be overused at times. I ask them, "How long were you with them for?" And the reply normally comes back as something like, "Ten years." I then ask, "Well, did you love them, or were they always a narcissist?" The answer usually is, "I loved them for eight or nine years, and then suddenly, they changed and became a narcissist." My question I always ask back is, "Is it possible that there was something in them that you saw, that if you truly reflected back in a true heart-like manner, you can now see that the same trait that really upset you is actually in you as well, and perhaps you didn't want to acknowledge that flaw on a conscious level?" Because as I said already, the people who come into our lives mirror back the areas we need to self-improve on ourselves. We attract them energetically on the subconscious level, so that we can become better versions of ourselves. Or our vibe attracts our tribe i.e. like attracts like. Sometimes, we are consciously aware and accept this, and other times, we deny it and never change. This is why sometimes, people attract the same kind of partner again and again. It is interesting that the word "partner" and the word "parent" have exactly the same letters, except there is an extra "r" in partner, so you replay the parent relationship sometimes until you heal those stuck emotions. Once you become aware and heal these traits, then the lesson is no longer needed, and you will hopefully not attract another one. So next time instead of attracting lessons, you will attract a love.

I will say that the word narcissist in terms of an acronym in some cases can mean:

Neglected

Awareness

Reflecting

Conditionings

In

Suppressed

Self

Instigating

Soul

Transition.

In other words, these people come into our lives to help release these suppressed emotions from traumas in childhood that we have tucked away at the back of the heart or the subconscious and haven't truly released them. Or these narcissists are there to help us become more emotionally intelligent, so that we can deal with people like this in an easier fashion in the future. All I say is if you attracted a narcissist, so ask yourself why, without playing the victim and without pointing the finger. Truly go into your heart space and ask, "Why?"

The third part of the exercise, is like the TV program "Who Wants to Be a Millionaire." When you are stuck on an answer, you have the option to phone a friend and ask for help or their opinion. In this last part, find someone you trust and who will be brutally honest with you and not hold anything back. Then, ask them to tell you all the things they see in you that they do not like and all the things they think are holding you back in life. I did this exercise with my dad, who is probably my biggest critic, and he told me to bring the biggest notepad I could possibly find! My word, did he have a lot to say! Anyway, moving swiftly on, make sure you also tell the person that you are doing the exercise to self-improve and you will take your ego completely out of the situation and look back into conversation with no emotion and no intention of retorting. Say that you are doing the exercise to self-improve and they are doing you a favor by being so honest. Tell them when finished, you will either thank them if on the phone or give them a hug or handshake in gratitude for their help. Make sure you write everything down, and add it to your master list. Be conscious, though, that some of the things they list may be mirroring back in the reflection they see in you. Despite this, own the traits anyway, as you may energetically help them by doing so as well.

On a side note; on this point, you might find after doing this exercise properly, you will change for the better, but the people in your family and friends circle may still see you as the old person they remember you as. You may have released those old programs, but they may project their old perception of you, onto you. This is where it is very important to stand in your own power and in your new state of awareness, and understand that it may take time for them to see your change, so be patient. You never know, your changes may affect positive change in them as well. So, stay strong, and stay on the path.

Going back to the exercise, by now you will have a comprehensive list of your self-aware programs that don't serve you, your mirrored programs, and your phone-a-friend or third-party programs, giving you a great list to work on.

Once you have this list, then go and get a coach, a psychologist, or a trusted friend to work with you. This is paramount, and the reason being is the next part of the exercise is to voice these traits out loud with absolute passion, with your hand on your heart and an energy and intention in terms of it being a ceremony to release them all. By voicing out loud, you are firstly expressing awareness and then acceptance that these traits are in you, in order to allow the process of change. This is so important because if you are not aware of the flaws in the first place, how can you work on them or get rid of them? Likewise, even if someone makes you aware but you don't accept that they are in you, you can't change. I'm sure at some stage of your life, you have had a parent or a loved one say, "You are so stubborn," or maybe, "You are so lazy," in terms of a trait they see in you, and you have refused to believe it is in you at all, and they must be seeing things. Then, although someone has made you aware, you ignore them and keep on living that flaw. So, this is why having true awareness and acceptance is paramount for change. And the reason it is so important to voice these traits out loud is the same reason they do it in support groups like Alcoholics Anonymous, where they say, "I am an alcoholic, but I accept that and am willing to change." By saying it out-loud in front of other people, you are triggering three different parts of the brain, including the subconscious, to create that awareness and acceptance to allow the change. So, for example, with your hand on your heart and with true passion, you might say, "At times, I don't actively listen enough, but I accept that and I am willing to change. At times, I get egotistical, but I accept that and am willing to change. At times, I get distracted, but I accept that and am willing to change." I'm sure you get the picture, yes? The other reason for voicing it outloud with someone is that you have them to keep you accountable, and this can help you change more quickly and with more focused action. There were some traits I didn't even realize I had in me before doing this exercise, and since completion of the exercise, the awareness has helped me implement massive change.

Once you have gone through your entire list voicing out-loud with passion and purpose, take that piece of paper and rip it up into shreds and feel with intention, the energy of those traits going away. Then, throw the pieces of paper on a fire, burning them, blow them up or flush them down a toilet, finally getting rid of all that energy that you had held on to. Really feel like it's a spiritual, mental, and emotional ritual. I do this in corporations and have teams of people rip the pieces of paper up and trek down to the toilets to flush away those traits that haven't served them. It's amazing to watch some people return to the meeting room afterwards as though two bricks have been removed from their shoulders; they immediately feel lighter and happier.

Once you have completed these steps, the next exercise is to take another piece of paper and write down all the opposites of the traits you just read out and write them as positive "I am" statements. So, for example, if we were to take the trait of not actively listening, you would write, "I am always actively listening with love and understanding to the other person's perspective." Or if we wanted to take the egotistical one, you would write, "I am always humble and kind," or something to that extent. Once you have written all of these positive statements down, then twice a day for a minimum of 21 days—but preferably 60 days—say these out-loud, with passion and purpose, with your coach or friend or in front of a mirror, with your hand on your heart and looking directly into your own eyes. By doing this, you will speak out-loud these positive affirmations or mantras to your subconscious and implement positive change over time through neuroplasticity within the

Brain, and in turn, almost hypnotically create new character traits in your psyche. Keep your awareness on how your change and watch yourself on a daily basis.

Once you have done the initial task, you can journal at the end of the day as an exercise to keep on top of your changes. One way of doing this is before you go to bed, look at all your interactions you had during the day and all the situations you were in, whether interacting with others or even your own self in terms of self-talk and contemplation. Then through a state of reflection and awareness, write down the thoughts, the behaviors, and the emotions you had in those circumstances, and write down what served you and what held you back in those situations and interactions. Then, write down, if you had been the perfect God-like version of yourself in that interaction, what emotions would have been the best placed to feel at that point in time(hopefully joy, happiness, or love as some examples), what behaviors would have served you best in that situation, and finally, what thoughts would have served you the best to create those behaviors and emotions you wanted. If you do this on a regular basis, you will create self-awareness to allow self-improvement and positive change. Remember, though, it is like going to the gym; you need to be consistent and disciplined every day to build up those neuro-muscles within your psyche. Keep going for at least 21 days, and see if you notice a change. You can add in some visualization meditation exercises if you like, to see yourself in those situations in the future, acting out the best way to create win-win in all aspects of life.

When I did this entire exercise myself, I felt a massive shift of energy and I actually was in tears. You might say I was not very manly, but being able to show your vulnerability and admit your imperfections is one of the greatest gifts you can give yourself. Plus, some of the most successful people in the world have a sense of humility. Even one of my toughest male coaching clients, had the same impactful experience as I did. He was a six-foot-four ex-professional American footballer, and I had him in my office. He was incredibly strong physically and mentally, but when he released his parental programs that he hadn't even been aware of, there was a massive emotional shift in him, and that brought him to tears. It was beautiful to see, and I felt a bonded connection with him and an admiration for him during the experience. He was strong enough to admit his flaws, and that, in my viewpoint, is pretty impressive, especially in the masked communities we have on social media, where people are hiding their true selves. He actually paid me thousands of dollars to work with him in respect to coaching, but once we had done this exercise, he said he didn't need to come back. I offered him his money back on a pro rata basis, but he said what I had done was worth every single dollar. Have the intention that the exercise is going to be a game-changer; do it with meaning and passion, and then, continue to do the positive re-programming every day with consistency and discipline. This is key. Remember this is an exercise of self-love and improving emotional intelligence for yourself. If you feel you need to do it again; go for it, make it fun, and make it almost like a game.

Once you have completed the entire exercise properly, it can have an amazing positive effect on you and the people around you. You will have raised your awareness, and your energetic frequency will be positively higher. It will also make you a better person, and the people around you will feel it. Imagine if everyone in a business did this as well—it would be so powerful. Less conflict, less worry, less stress, and less distractions through unnecessary interactions. It would mean you and your staff being more focused on your missions and goals, rather than your problems and worries. Gossip and time wasting could be eliminated. The most successful leaders in business and in life tend to be the most emotionally intelligent, so working on this can help you in all of the interactions of life. Imagine being able to keep calm and rational in negotiations, in peer reviews, when getting told off, or when someone makes a mistake in some form. It will save you energy and keep you in a balanced state, which means better decision-making as well. Most of all, though, it clears out the old stuck emotions and baggage, allowing you to feel more positive in life.

I did this exercise with a business owner of two companies: a large computer hardware firm and a manufacturing engineering company. He had set a target to be involved in some kind of merger or acquisition deal, to expand his companies. The week after he had completed the awareness exercise and we had done some manifestation affirmations together, a large British company offered to buy out his entire computer hardware business for millions of euros. That same week, he was separately offered an engineering company at a very low price to help expand his engineering business, where the owner of another similar business was retiring, and this owner wanted to pass on his legacy to someone he knew would appreciate it and continue on the good name and service. I believe this came from aligning his energy to a higher state in order to attract his wishes and dreams super-fast.

# THE POWER OF LETTING GO TO BE YOUR BEST SELF

In the previous chapter, we did the awareness exercise, in order to get rid of parental programs, triggers, and traits that don't serve you. When you have tension in the body from holding onto emotions such as anger, resentment, lack of forgiveness, or guilt, they can drain the body of energy or cause you to get easily triggered and distracted. This is low vibration energy and is certainly something you do not want when you are looking to create your best self energetically and perform at the highest level. It can be likened to buying an old house which has good foundations but just hasn't been cared for and the owner has left a load of rubbish inside. The awareness exercise that I described is likened to stripping that house down, clearing out all the rubbish, redecorating it to look fantastic, and maybe even redesigning it to be a better house all round. Sometimes, it can have a massive positive impact on your energy levels as well as releasing blockages within. In a personal sense, it can help you focus on your fabulous future, rather than the problems of the past.

In other words to ensure optimal mindset you need to let go of any anger, resentment towards others, or guilt you may hold inside yourself for something you have done. This is where forgiveness and understanding for others or oneself is key. One of the biggest energy blocks that people can have is a lack of forgiveness for someone who did something to them in the past or something they did themselves to others. It can literally hold a person back in life and affect their mindset in such a negative way. It is so important to let go and forgive others, in all circumstances, not necessarily for them, but for you and your own wellbeing. Not forgiving someone leaves a grudge, and this isn't good for you either in a business or in a love relationship. A grudge is like a stuck emotion or a stuck "energy in motion" within the body, and that cannot be good for the body. That energy will vibrate out of sync from the body's usual vibrational energy, and over time, it can cause dis-harmony within the body cells and in turn cause a state of dis-ease, which could lead to disease.

There are two well-known exercises I would recommend for releasing this and allowing forgiveness. The first is to write a letter to the person. You don't necessarily have to send it, you can just write it and get the energy out of you and onto paper. Tell them all the things they did to you that upset you and then tell them you forgive them for each and every one. Or, if you did something to someone else and you need to forgive yourself, you can write them a letter saying there is no intention of anything other than to say you are grateful for the relationship you had or have with them, and you apologize with true meaning for any upset you caused. If you want you can send it, do, or if the person you are forgiving has passed away, you can always burn it in a ceremony.

One lady I had on my radio show went to forgive her father's killer. The killer was part of the IRA in Northern Ireland, and 16 years before she met him, he had let off a bomb in a hotel where her father was staying, and he was killed. When the lady met with the killer, she realized he got into the IRA just to support his town, his country, and his political views. She forgave him, and once he realized what a good person she was, he was truly sorry. Her empathy, compassion, and forgiveness completely disarmed him, and they went on to become partners in trying to bring peace to areas of the world where there was conflict. They would go on stage together talking about how through empathy, they were able to understand each other's perspective, viewpoints, and opinions, in order to realize how important it truly is to seek to understand others before making judgements and assumptions.

The second forgiveness exercise I learned from Louise Hay, who wrote a fantastic book called *You Can Heal Your Life*. She is a truly amazing woman who changed so many lives for the positive. I have adapted her technique, but it is pretty much the same.

1. While standing, cup your hands, facing upwards, in front of your heart, as if you were holding water in your cupped hands.

2. Imagine a six-inches-tall, five-year-old version of yourself standing on your cupped hands in front of your heart. The reason for the five-year-old version is that back then, you were generally in a state of innocence with little or no ego. It can also represent your inner child. The main aim, though, is to have no judgement towards that little child, towards you.

3. Then, say to your innocent, younger self with true meaning, "I love you, I forgive you, I am sorry, and I let it go." Then, put your imaginary five-year-old self into your heart and visualize the love you have for him or her within. You might ask, "Why do I need to forgive myself?" Let's face it: in a love relationship scenario, you chose to go into that relationship, so you are responsible as well.

4. Next, cup your hands again in the same way in front of your heart, and this time, imagine the five-year-old version of the person you need to forgive.

5. Again, this time to the person you are forgiving, say, "I love you, I forgive you, and I let it go," and put them into your heart and

imagine your younger innocent self and their younger self in a platonic embrace of love, or a hug.

This sounds either hard or silly, but I did this myself with my ex-wife for something she did to me, and the next day after doing the exercise, she rang up and apologized to me and said we have two amazing kids and we need to be friends for them. It's a powerful technique that even the most non-spiritual CEOs that I worked with said it changed their lives, as they were able to forgive their fathers, mothers, exes, or even an old colleague. I have also done this forgiveness technique on stage with audience members coming up at different events and doing the exercise while I guided them. Quite often, when they forgive their own self, they are loving and kind in their tone of voice, but when it comes to the person they are forgiving, sometimes, it can be very funny, as you can hear they are saying they forgive, but really, the energy is still saying that the other person is a total asshole and that will not energetically work. There can be no masks nor pretending—to forgive, you must really mean it with love and authenticity.

Often, when we forgive ourselves or others for the past, we can release anger, resentment, and guilt. It can be massively beneficial to you and your body and again can release trigger points. This will mean if you have a similar interaction in the future, you can be more emotionally aware and controlled. It also really helps to have a true understanding of the other person's perspective and understand that they come from a different background and upbringing, and that means that sometimes, they just see and interpret a situation differently from you. So, if you have a future interaction that is stressful and testing, instead of reacting, do the Navy Seal box breathing technique where you breathe in for four seconds, hold the breath for four seconds, breathe out for four seconds, hold the breath out for four seconds, and then repeat this process four times. This exercise calms the central nervous system down and will give you a chance to pause, relax your emotions, and respond, rather than react, giving the best response, which normally is to ask questions to understand. Quite often, we make assumptions, rather than knowing the reality of what the other person is thinking.

The awareness and forgiveness techniques will also help you reduce the amount of negative thoughts you have, as you will have got rid of a lot of trigger points and character traits, such as judgment and envy. Despite this, certain past experiences and trauma can still bring negative thoughts into people's heads at times. We all have that little voice sometimes telling us we are not good enough or we are not worthy, or this idea won't work. It's just whether you choose to listen to that voice or listen to your heart and the positive voice instead. In terms of voices in our head we hear, I do believe, that some people who are psychic can tap into energy waves within the atmosphere, and if sensitive, they can pick up on other people's negative

Thoughts around them. An exercise to help with getting rid of negative thoughts in a fun way is the following:

Imagine that as a child, you came into the world with no negative thoughts at all. You were innocent, and for the first few years of your life, the only thing you thought about was food, pooping, and hugs. Then, your brother, sister, cousin, mum or dad annoyed you in some way, and these negative thoughts came into play. So, in one way, you can say that you came into this world as a beacon of love and light, and then your energy field got disrupted by other people messing with your peace. In other words, negative thoughts were initiated from outside of you. Shamen Durek, who has a fantastic book called Spirit Hacking, talked about this on stage. You could say to a kid who is having problems, with negative thoughts or to yourself; to imagine all negative thoughts are like "dementors" in other words those eerie ghosts in the film Harry Potter that drain your energy. Imagine these dementors are low frequency beings and see you as a channel of light; and the reason why they are coming to you is they just want to get back to the light. Almost a bit like Luke Skywalker in Star Wars turning his father, Darth Vader, back from the dark side of the force to the good side. Likewise, these dementors want to have their low frequency energy turned back into high frequency positive energy. So, make it a game and send them there. If you get a negative thought, say to the dementor (i.e. the gamified negative thought), "Dementor, I am a being of light, like Luke Skywalker. I only think positive thoughts, so if you are here in my mind, you must want to go to the light, so I am going to send you there," and then, in your mind's eye, see the dementor or negative thought go up to the light with love. Once you can visualize the dementor or negative thought in the light, then say, "Dementor, now that you are in the light, you must only have positive thoughts for me." And what you are doing here is energetically setting the intention to receive a positive thought. Then, once you have received a positive thought, thank the dementor, and then, in your mind's eye, see it disappearing into the light. I often use violet light in my visualization, as violet is the highest frequency of light. So, what this exercise does is to gamify negative thoughts and gives you a fun way of turning them into positive thoughts. If you are giving this exercise to a child, you can also tell them that they can count up how many dementors they convert into positive thoughts each day and maybe points can equal prizes, which is even more fun! This way, you are changing the whole energy around negative thoughts into a fun game, reframing and increasing positivity. You are also giving them a sense of purpose of turning the darkness into light, making them feel good and, in turn, changing their state further towards the positive.

    Another tactic to deal with negative thoughts is every time you get one, stop yourself in your tracks and say out loud, (as long as no one else is around, otherwise you will look a bit bonkers, as if you are talking to yourself) say, "Really? Is that my truth?" And what you are doing here is catching that negative voice or ego out consciously, showing that you hold the inner power to know that you are good enough or you can succeed. Once you have done this, think of something that you are grateful for to take you out of the energy of negativity and into the energy of positivity. So, for example, for me, I like to think of when I first held my son and my daughter in my hands when they were born as a gratitude trigger to get me back into the energy of positivity. You can obviously come up with your own; it could be winning a race in school, a hug from your mum or dad, or your wedding day. Whatever triggers you into happiness as a memory, use it. This is a good tactic in business as well. When you are just about to pitch for some new business, go back into the memory of a time when you won some previous business successfully. Get into that energetic feeling, and then go in and make your pitch with that same energy and confidence. Watch the magic that will happen.

# HOW TO TURN YOUR MESS INTO A MESSAGE AND GIVE IT MEANING

During my time in the investment world, I had the honor and pleasure of meeting thousands of amazingly successful people. These people included C-level executives all the way to heart-warming receptionists. When you first met them, they always had a smile and seemed superhuman in terms of their professionalism and perfection. However, once we became friends and they opened up, it was obvious we are all the same— we all have stresses, anxieties, and worries in life, and if left as stuck emotions or energy within, these can affect the body in a negative way and can also cause triggers in people, which doesn't add value to them in business or in life relationships.

I said earlier that everything is energy and that we create energetically through our thoughts, our words, and our actions. When I used to pitch my investment products for example to clients, I would often voice out loud, "We invest using a top down, bottom up investment process"— sounds flash, doesn't it? Well, I do wish I hadn't said that, as I truly believe that every word we use and every sentence we say can energetically create outcomes. Sometimes, the sentences we say can be the sentences we condemn ourselves and others to, or our word is our wand, so be careful what you say as your words can magically create. In

2008, when stock and property markets fell there were a lot of stressed people out there, and I was one of them. In 2009, after various stress-related ailments, I had cameras bottom up and top down inside my body. I eventually needed an operation on my digestive system— which was in fact my ass, if I am honest— and this didn't go well, and I then needed another operation to correct the damage of the first one, which didn't go well either. This led to pain in the abdomen from 2009 to 2012. It was so bad that I was waking up sometimes 10 times in the night with pain like I was being punched in the stomach. I also had pain in the daytime, and sometimes, I would have to excuse myself in the middle of meetings to go to the bathroom, as this pain was so excruciating. The pain was so bad. I tried everything, even put deep heat cream and imada hotdrug oil up my backside. It was that bad. This led to massive stress, anxiety, depression, and eventually, to my marriage breaking down. Then, at the end of 2012, when the Mayans had predicted that the world would come to an end, mine almost did. I ended up getting a stomach bug called the norovirus, and after ten days of serious dehydration, where I was literally sprint training to the toilet, while performing butt clenching techniques, while running to ensure an element of mess retention, my electrolytes went down to virtually zero, and I was rushed to hospital in an ambulance with chest pain. The ECG said a heart issue and my blood pressure had doubled, and I thought I was toast. As I was rushed from accident and emergency to X-ray, I was shaking with fear. The pain in my chest was so intense, and I was finding it hard to breath. I felt on the edge; I wasn't sure I was going to make it. I prayed I would see my kids again. I prayed and said if I came through this, I would dedicate my life in some way to helping others. I suddenly blanked out and was encapsulated by this amazing feeling of love, energy, and connection, nothing like I felt before. If you take your best orgasm and multiply it by a hundred times all over your body, especially in your heart, you might just get the feeling. I was having a near-death experience. I felt like I was connected to everything, and everything was just energy interconnected, and I was surrounded by a feeling of absolute love. There was no man with a beard, but there was a conscious, loving energy there, and I got a knowing that I needed to change my life in some way or form. Obviously, I survived. Otherwise, I wouldn't be writing to you now. Following this experience, I changed my life. I looked back, and I realized I had been developing stomach issues even before 2008. I realized it was my body telling me I was not aligned to my true sense of purpose or I hadn't created a true sense of purpose in what I was doing. I had been living from a place of ego, and I had just seen my job as all about money and greed. I could have reframed it into a sense of making lives better in some way or form, but that was a lesson I had to learn. I quickly recovered in the hospital, and the doctors were astonished by my quick turnaround.

Following the near-death experience, I was determined to give something back, as promised, and I went and did something called the 'Alpha course', which is a Christian church course that Bear Gryles, the famous TV adventurer had done. I thought if it's good enough for an ex-SAS army guy, then surely good enough for me. Funnily enough, I ended up meeting and chatting with Bear at a conference in 2020. Proof of energy in action again! Anyway, the first time I turned up at the course, they were very pushy in terms of Jesus and God. I said to them I definitely believed in a higher source and definitely believed in Jesus, let's face it, there are millions of books written about him, however, I found it hard to believe that Jesus was the one and only son of God. Yes, I felt he was a prophet, yes, I felt he was the closest thing on earth to God (apart from the likes of Buddha, Krishna, Allah, Mohammed, and a few others). However, I felt that we were all sons and daughters of God and all have the potential to be God-realized. I said to them that I felt all religions are like rivers to the sea; they are all beautiful paths to the sea, that being God or Allah or whoever you believe in, but the main aim is to get to the sea, and I wasn't sure which path was the best for me. Anyway, at this point, the Alpha teachers were wondering what I was doing there, and I went away thinking I wasn't going to go back.

This was a Monday and I walked out and looked up to the heavens and said, "God, Universe, please give me a sign to tell me whether I should go back and do that course?" Two days after my encounter at the Alpha course, I was helping one of my friends and clients with nutritional advice for cancer. He had gone through some pretty stressful times at work and had unfortunately picked up prostate cancer. Anyway, having had some digestive issues myself in the past, I had researched intensively into the nutritional and alternative treatment side of cancer of the bowels or prostate area.

We were chatting through various things he had tried, and out of the blue, I said to him, "Chris, we have tried a lot of different nutritional tips to help in terms of body-orientated healing. In terms of soul-like healing, have you considered church as a way to find peace within and reduce stress?" He said that was an interesting idea, as they do always say that healing is a three-fold mix of body, mind, and soul. He had tried the nutritional body stuff and the mindful positive thinking and was still not succeeding. So perhaps it was time to try some soulfulness as well.

That evening, when I returned home from work, I decided it was time to go out and have a run, which was common practice for myself as a premier league hockey player for my local club. That evening, I decided to take the dog with me, as we regularly ran together.

Never before had the dog tripped me up, however, while running at full pace, for no reason, the dog suddenly cut across me. I went flying over her and landed with an almighty crash on my right side with my hand and knee getting the full brunt of it. Blood was all over the place, and it wasn't stopping. I couldn't run on, so my only choice was to turn around and hobble home as quickly as possible. When I walked through the door with blood everywhere, my ex-wife had a fit; she wondered what on earth had I done. Once the bleeding had stopped, we were suddenly drawn to looking at the shapes of the cuts. On first inspection, we saw there were two "8"s or infinity signs on my hand and one on my knee. "888"—lucky it wasn't "666," my ex-wife joked! I said isn't that the Chinese lucky number? I wonder if I am going to win the lottery I laughed! My ex-wife then joked and said to look more closely and see if there were any more numbers. There were no numbers, however, between the two infinity signs on my hand were the letters 'INri'. I didn't even know what it meant, however, my ex-wife, who is an Irish Catholic knew exactly those letters from the cross of Jesus. Usually seen in capitals, they were Roman initials standing for "Jesus of Nazareth, King of the Jews" in Latin. Now I know this sounds far-fetched, however, I have photographs and physically showed as many people as possible. I could get three vicars and around one hundred people to verify they had seen it. I showed it to every client I met, and they were all amazed.

I was awestruck. I didn't know what to think. Automatically, I went into an ego perspective; "I must be Jesus" I thought, yes, that's it: I am Jesus reincarnated, and I have a mission to do. Then, humility kicked in—or should I say my ex-wife gave me a clip around the ear and told me to get with the program. It was much more likely a sign from God or the Universe to get back and do that Alpha course. In fact, the first two letters were in capitals and the last two lower case. So, it was almost like a message saying "Jesus of Nazareth here, not really king of the Jews, but go back and do that course," so I did. On a side note, one thing I did find funny after reflection of this is that my son, who, was born in 2005, is called Joshua, and that is the English version of Jesus' real Hebrew name, "Yeshua." Also, my daughter, who is called Sarah, was born in 2008, and in the gnostic bibles, which are the texts that didn't make it into the final versions of the Bible, they say that Jesus was actually married and had a daughter called Sarah. Kind of cool considering and

I had no idea of either fact when we were choosing names. Now Jesus having a child may sound far-fetched, but if you think about it, there is nothing written about Jesus between the ages of 13 and 30 in the Bible, and in those times, middle class Jews were generally married by the time they were 18. Jesus was a confident speaker, great communicator, loving, caring, and intelligent man, so I am sure he would have not been short of interested parties. Plus, if God or any divine being was to come down to experience the gift of living in this physical state, would it not be natural to want to experience love in this form? Love is the highest form of connection between two human beings, and the Bible preaches about God and Creation. So, why not create another human being through an act of love while in physical form.

So, naturally, after this fall and branding on my hand, I was both amazed, and a bit freaked out. I truly believe that the Universe or our own energetic resonance sends us signs or we attract them based on our energy frequency to guide us on our path in life; you just need to be awake and aware to spot them. This one obviously didn't need much spotting. The following week, I was back at the course, showing everyone my cuts and as enthusiastic as ever. Suddenly, I was a total convert and started reading the Bible and as much around the subject of the bible as possible. On the tenth week of the Alpha course, there was an away day where you go to a church and spend time talking and learning all about the Holy Spirit. It was a lovely day and at the end of it, we took turns praying for each other one at a time. Imagine, you would have twenty people all praying for you at the same time. When it came to my go and they all started to pray for me, I suddenly felt this incredible warmth throughout my whole body and felt the brightest of lights shining in my eyes. I had them closed, so I opened them, expecting to see the sun shining in through one of the church windows. There was nothing. I closed my eyes again, and sure enough, the bright light came back as if I had an industrial torch shining in my face. I also suddenly felt this feeling of elation in my heart. It was one of the strangest, but loveliest experiences of my life. Half of me started wondering if I was having another near-death experience.

That evening, I had a late hockey match for my club. I am normally a highly competitive center forward, who really gives out a hundred percent and wants to win at all costs. But after this experience I had no aggression in me whatsoever. In fact, I would go as far as saying I felt angelic. It was a strange and lovely experience. I felt like having fun with all on the pitch, but with no intention of anything but love towards all. My teammates were asking me what on the earth was wrong? I could pass beautifully, run perfectly, play the game perfectly in a non-aggressive manner, but when it came to a fifty-fifty tackle, I didn't have my normal aggression.

After this experience, I was even more full-on a believer. I finished the Alpha course and then started going to church almost every day. I would go in between meetings, after work, twice on Sunday, and even started Bible classes. The church we went to was lovely; it was a New Age church called St. Paul's in Cheam, in Surrey in the U.K., and I thoroughly enjoyed it. They have a proper band, modern pop-like hymns, and people tend to sing and dance with their hands in the air. In fact, a lot of other churches should copy them; it would help bring in the crowds and make it fun. It should be about fun, community, and love, and the sessions should be modernized to entice new people in.

As time went on, I read more and more of the Bible and then started to read around the Bible, too, in terms of when the final copies were put together. I realized that some of the history and facts around the Christian faith and religion didn't get into the Bible, itself. I concluded that Christianity is a lovely route to the divine, and to inner peace, however, I felt it was important to understand different perspectives of the same thing. I have said it before, and I will say it again; we all come from different backgrounds and perspectives in life, and it is so important to seek to ask the right questions to understand the other people's views, rather than just pushing your own opinions on others. That means we all are brought up differently and experience life differently, and that includes different religions because of the differing life perspectives. I decided to study other religions as well, to get a different viewpoint from others around the world. I felt it would be arrogant to think that my route was the only route to the divine. Buddhism, Islam, Hinduism, Judaism, Sikhism, Taoism. They are all beautiful routes to God or the Universal energy or Allah or Krishna or whatever you believe in. I realize now that religions are like rivers to the sea, the sea being the divine. Each can be a beautiful route, and none of them are wrong; they are all just different paths to a very similar belief, in my opinion. This is how I got into spirituality and then became a master teacher healer of five modalities of healing and a meditation coach. To be honest, it was to heal myself to begin with, but then I discovered I could help others as well. After the healing, I realized the importance of the mind-body connection and how thoughts are energy and that they can affect you on the physical level. I was able to heal myself through the realization that the spiritual, mental, emotional, and physical sides of us are all interlinked, and by working on all areas, you can heal yourself properly and get yourself into the best state. In order to widen my skillset to help more people, I went on to become a mindset, performance, and executive coach and also a certified mental wellness practitioner. Since then, I have been using my knowledge and experiences to support and inspire others to a different way of thinking and to achieve whatever they need in life. I mix psychological performance-enhancing knowledge with a spiritual knowing and understanding of how to optimize energy to optimize your life.

On top of this, one of my greatest gifts after the near-death experience was a heightened intuitive sense of being able to read people's thoughts and energy. This really helps in deciphering what they need in life in order to help them quickly, whether in business, in their relationships, or with their health.

For over ten years now, I have been mixing a business side and a Buddha side. I am not a Buddhist per say, but it is one of the religions I really love, and the phrase encapsulates my business and holistic work. On the business side, I have spoken on stages all over the globe, done corporate training, coaching, and consulting in some of the largest companies in the world, like Dell, for example. Then, on my Buddha side, I have been doing life coaching, healing, and mental wellness work, helping people release and let go of the emotions and pains that do not serve them and helping them turn their mess into a message and give it meaning to help other people and give them a sense of purpose.

I have a real-life story to showcase and highlight the use of the awareness and forgiveness exercises I went through earlier and how powerful they can be in changing someone's mindset even in the worst circumstances you can imagine.

In early 2022 I was on a virtual stage talking about mental wellness where we had a mix of psychologists, psychiatrists, neuroscientists, mindset coaches, and mental wellness practitioners helping out people who came onto the stage or into the virtual room supporting them with stress, anxiety, depression, suicidal tendencies, and other mental health conditions. We did this virtual stage on a weekly basis for five hours at a time and once a month for twelve hours. It would usually finish at 1 a.m. my time.

This one girl from the Maldives named Yao came into the room and onto the stage. She told us that she had been in bed for three days, had no food for two days, and no water for over 24 hours. She told us she was suicidal. Naturally, everyone on the panel was very worried and were sending messages in the back channel asking if we should contact the Maldives authorities or the virtual app authorities and try and get her help. There were questions such as; did she have family, who could help her? or friends who could support her? She said there was no one. She told us she had been in an abusive marriage with a narcissistic sociopath who had sexually, emotionally, and physically abused her for their entire marriage, which had only ended a couple of years ago. She also had been sexually abused as a thirteen-year-old when she had been drugged and raped. She was suffering massively from trauma and was very depressed. Some of this information she told us then and there, and some I found out later. We were deeply worried, and no one knew how to handle the situation.

I sat there and went into my heart space, and connected with my inner self, and said out loud with a true sense of love, "How can I help this woman?" The message that came into my head, was to change her state as quickly as possible. Make her smile, even laugh, and get her to drink water as soon as possible. Suddenly, it came to me. I got into a knowing state. I didn't think it would work; I didn't believe it would work; I just knew it would work. So, I said to her, "Yao, do you enjoy playing games?" And after a slight hesitation, she said, "Yes." I replied, "Well, if you play a fun game with me, which I guarantee you will win, I will give you a prize worth over $1,500." She asked me what the prize was, and I said it was a free mindset coaching and mental wellness consultation with me. She was crying out for help and was delighted. The next thing I did, you might think was a bit risky with a suicidal girl, but I just knew it was the right thing to do; I could feel it in my heart. I said to her, "Yao, for fun, I want to hear how loud you can gargle on this stage with water. In fact, let's see if you can become the clubhouse gargle champion. Are you up for a bit of fun?" After a little hesitation, she agreed. So, for the first time in three days, she got out of bed, and for the first time in 24 hours, she got a glass of water. I said to her, "Right, Yao, just to check the audio on the microphone is working, can you gulp down a mouthful of water, just to check that we can hear you properly?" This was just a tactic to get her to drink straight away, and sure enough, she agreed. I pretended I didn't really hear the first gulp and asked her to do another one, which she did. I then told her to do her first gargle, and off she went. At this point,

I started to cheer her on and shouted with fun, encouragement, and enthusiasm, "Come on girl!! you can do better than that! Let's really hear that gargle." She gargled louder and louder and then began to laugh. I was so grateful she had changed her state. So, after six gargles and six big gulps of water, we had the whole stage clapping and cheering, and she was laughing herself. Massive relief was felt in the messages in the back channel. I then said to her, "Yao, you are fantastic, you are a superstar. I am so impressed and so delighted for you becoming the new clubhouse gargle champion. You have won the prize with me, but will you do one last thing for me which again is easy and you will like it?" She agreed. I said, "Would you go into the kitchen and get a piece of bread if you have it," which she did. "Now that you have the slice of bread in your hand, will you take a really good look in gratitude for the bread and realize that that piece of bread started as seeds that were planted in the ground by a farmer and sowed into wheat, the wheat was then harvested and made into flour, then the flour into bread and then delivered to the shop where you were able to buy it from, and now provide nutrition and sustenance for your body. I want you to have that awareness and have gratitude for the bread and the people who have labored over it. I want you to look at the bread in gratitude, I want you to take a bite with gratitude, I want you to feel the bread in your mouth with gratitude, I want you to hear the bread in your mouth with gratitude, I want you to taste it with gratitude, and I want you to swallow the bread with gratitude. The reason I want you to do this, is to show that if you can be grateful for the simplest of things in life like a piece of bread, then you can start to show gratitude for all the small things you have in life, such as the bed you sleep in, the roof over your head, the food you eat, and the family you have. Then, through the feeling of gratitude, you will bring contentment to your heart for the things and the people you have in your life already, however small. This will then open your subconscious up to make you feel worthy enough to receive more good things into your life." She did this, took several bites, and felt much better.

So, in a very short period of time, she went from depression and suicide to getting out of bed, drinking, laughing, and eating. I had helped her in changing her state—and according to the lead panelist in the room, saved her life. I exchanged numbers with her over messages and within 36 hours, we were on a Zoom call together. Before the call, I checked in with her on text a few times, to show love and care and more importantly, to gain her trust before the session.

During the session, she went into much more detail about her being sexually assaulted at thirteen, her mother not believing her, her father not being around, her abusive marriage, and then her depression and the fact that she had previously tried to attempt suicide. I again went into my heart space and realized I needed to carefully guide her and help her, in order to ensure she never attempted suicide again and to help her let go of the past so that she could move positively forward in life. I wanted to help her to forgive her ex-husband, the boy who sexually assaulted her, her mother for being controlling (and not believing all that happened to her), and her father for leaving the family when she was younger, not for them, but for her and her own wellbeing, so that she could let go of all those stuck emotions and move positively forward in her life. Then, I wanted to reframe her way of looking at these past hardships in her life, turning her mess into a message and give it meaning in order for her to help others with her story in the future. Thus, turning a traumatic past into a terrific sense of purpose.

Firstly, in terms of stopping her from attempting suicide again, I told her about my near-death experience and how I was encapsulated in this amazing feeling of love, energy, and connection, nothing like I'd ever felt before. I told her; that since my near-death experience, it is as if I have turned a radio dial or receiver on, in my head, and I seem to get insights and glimpses from a universal consciousness, or whatever you believe in. I went on to say that I believe that the body we are in is our vehicle we use to experience life in a physical way. The true us is the energy within, and that energy can never be dissipated; it just moves from one form to another, which was actually talked about by the famous scientist Einstein. So, I believe that we come down to this planet again and again and again, reincarnating as different people each time, so that we can get different perspectives of life. Also, so that we can learn to grow to evolve, to become better versions of ourselves. I believe that life is like a game, and we play this game of life again and again, learning from the hardships and experiences of life in order to grow and evolve and then use what we learn to help and teach others to be able to go through the same experiences in an easier fashion. By turning our hardships or messes into messages, so others can learn from them and in turn, go through the lessons with less fear and in a more conscious manner, so that they come out the other side aware of the lesson more quickly. So, based on that belief, I told her that when a person goes through a really hard time in their life, like she has, maybe she should take herself out of the energy and the emotion of being the victim and into the energy of being a victor, and pat herself on the back. Because, maybe she has been playing this game of life so often, testing herself to absolute ultimate, lifetime after lifetime, and seeing if she can really push herself to the limit in terms of these hardships and challenges in life, to see if she can get through them, grow from them, and come out the other side as a better version of herself. It could almost, be looked at, like a computer game, testing yourself at a higher level each lifetime to make the game of life more of a challenge. Then to use the learnings and turn them into lessons to help others who go through or have gone through the same thing. What we go through, we grow through, to glow through! So, based on this belief, I said to her, that just maybe her soul chose this life plan on purpose and she was meant to go through all of this to find a deeper sense of meaning and understanding of human behavior or life. And, if she was the one who chose this life, then if she was to give up and attempt suicide, she would only have to come back in another life to repeat the same lessons again, and it might be even harder the next time. So, why not get it out of the way in this lifetime and use these past learnings to inspire other people. Give the mess she went through meaning and turn it into a message to help others. I also said to her in a state of empathy and compassion that this did not take away from what the two men did to her, at all; they were disgusting acts by both parties, and I truly acknowledged her pain with love and compassion.

All I wanted to do was to take her out of the state of being a victim and go into a divine state of thinking and look back into the experiences as if she was an observer and a student of life coming from a place of pure love and as an eternal being who lives lifetime after lifetime. Then, to look back at the situation and try to understand why it happened to her through a spiritual perspective rather than just a human perspective. Thus, looking at why those men did what they did to her and what must have been done to them in their childhoods to cause them to be so hateful inside and so disturbed to do that to another human being. I told her the reason I wanted her to do this was so that she could reframe these experiences, let go of the trauma, and have an understanding and maybe even forgiveness for them both. I also emphasized that the forgiveness wasn't necessarily for them, it was for her, so that she could clear out these energies and emotions from within her, understand the lessons, and then move forward in her life in a positive way. I also wanted to ensure, that she never attracted that kind of energy into her life again. I said that, for her, to have gone through these horrific events in her life shows that on a spiritual level, she has a big mission here on earth to use her mess and turn it into a message. To use her story and her lessons learned and tell other people, especially other women, so that they will be inspired by the way she was able to forgive them, learn from the horrific experiences, and turn them into a positive; in terms of helping other people who have gone through similar abuse in the past. She was now in a state of knowing, a state where she felt that these traumas had happened to enable her to learn, to grow, and to evolve as a soul and then teach and inspire others in the future.

Remember though, it is very important to bring anyone who has been through trauma like this, to this point very carefully. You must show respect, empathy, and compassion for what they went through before you suggest techniques to reframe traumas. I will reiterate and repeat this, as it is so important to first show genuine empathy, compassion, and understanding that what she went through was horrific and in no way was I making little of how hard it was or has been.

So, now, having got her to this point, I said to her to think of the two men who did this to her and look at the experiences in a God-like fashion of love and understanding, that although in no way did it excuse them for what they did, but as I said before, maybe they were abused as children, maybe they were beaten, maybe they were so hurt inside that the only thing that they were able give out was hurt to others, because they were never loved. As people often say, "Sometimes, hurt people hurt people." Could she have forgiveness for them based on that perception? She said yes, and in fact, she told me that her ex-husband had been sexually abused by his uncle when he was only eight years of age. It just shows you how important parenting is. We learn from and model our parents or older relations, and this man had been sexually assaulted when he was a child. Again, not in any way lessening the things he did to Yao, but it was a way to give a perspective of why he would do such a thing. It was a way to help Yao understand and forgive him, and in doing so, she could let go of the trauma and move forward in her life. She was brilliant and she saw all of these ideas making lot of sense in higher perspective helping her to learn about why it happened, so that she was able to reframe it in her mind, in order to allow forgiveness.

We then went into the forgiveness techniques I have described earlier. She had loads of tears, a massive release, and her energy completely changed afterwards. She was so grateful. She now has a new lease on life and is currently telling her story to other women in order to help them release their traumas, as well. She is such a beautiful soul and an inspiring person who has managed to turn her mess into a message to help others and give her life meaning.

The lessons with Yao could be applicable to so many people, even your own self. Look back at the hardships you have had in your life; the relationships, even if in a smaller scale, that you thought were toxic and try to understand what might have caused that other person to be like that. Were they hurt or abused as a child, and can you forgive them or even just understand why they did it? It could even be in business with a boss or a colleague. Also, can you look back at those hard times and see how, when you reframe them, there was a learning that may have helped you become the person you are today. Or, maybe you have already used your experiences and learnings to help and inspire others to be able to get through similar situations more easily themselves. That is one of my viewpoints in terms of the meaning and purpose of life. Look for the learnings in everything, reframe the hardships, and next time you are having a confrontation with someone, ask yourself, "Why is this happening to me, what is mirroring back in this interaction, how can I learn from this interaction, and what can I take from it to help others or myself in the future in some way or form? It allows you to almost gamify life into an opportunity to grow as a human being. I said it earlier that I believe the most successful people in life are the most emotionally intelligent and that emotional intelligence is probably the most grounded version of consciousness.

As I have stated already; one of the meanings of life, in my opinion, is that we can go through all these hardships, all these interactions, all these experiences, to see if we can become even more conscious or emotionally intelligent through the learnings and then teach what we learn to others in terms of turning your mess into a message to give it meaning.

You can reframe life to be like a PlayStation game or a computer game, where we test ourselves to the ultimate to see if we can come out the other side of all this crap as the best version of ourselves. Maybe the harder it is, the more times you have been playing the game of life. So, maybe if you are having a hard time in life, maybe pat yourself on the back, because just maybe you are such an evolved soul, you are pushing yourself that little extra bit to see if you can still win the game and be a good person and a good leader in respect to helping others, despite all these tests. And for those who find it too hard and do something like taking their own life, I believe they will only have to come down and repeat the same life experiences all over again, and it might be even more testing next time, so why not get it out of the way in this lifetime, learn the lessons or correct the karma, and move on in your overall soul life to the next level.

Realistically, if we are playing this game of life as a spiritual being experiencing a physical existence, surely, we would want to experience all senses of physicality such as pain and pleasure, the goods and the bad, and the successes and the failures, everything. When someone wins the lottery and gets a load of money without truly going through the work to get there, they often don't appreciate it, and often, the lottery winner has spent or lost all their money in a short space of time, if they are not conscious about it. This is why in life, if you have gone through tough times in the past, you can really and truly appreciate the good times when you come out the other end. The Ying and the Yang as they call it. You tend to appreciate the light so much more when you can differentiate it from the darkness.

It's also lovely when you go through these experiences and they lead you to finding your true purpose or create purpose around what you do from the experiences you have had. That sense of purpose will align and optimize your energy on the spiritual, mental, emotional, and physical sides of you, and if you optimize your energy, you will optimize your performance in life, in your relationships, and in your work.

Sometimes, when we are in the emotions of a situation, it can be difficult to see the wood from the trees, and people can get wrapped up trying to cure all the symptoms, rather than going to the source of the problem. For example, there was a person I knew who became addicted to gaming in terms of playing computer games too much every day. He had developed this addiction after his mum died when he was a young teenager. It must have been so tough for him, and my heart goes out to him. He was using gaming as a way of escaping reality, escaping the grief, rather than facing it and working through it. It is very common. Eventually, he managed to break the addiction, and later on in his adult life, he decided to turn his mess into a message to help kids and adults with gaming addictions. A very admirable cause. The only thing I would say is that his focus was still on the gaming, which was a symptom, rather than the true source which for him for example was dealing with grief. Find the source and you solve the need for the escape.

This is often similar in the medical world. I remember back in 2010, after my operations that went wrong and I was getting stomach pain, I went to see a specialist. He wanted to prescribe a form of anti-depressants to help numb the pain of the colon. This was only tackling a symptom. The real source of the problem was stress, and instead of taking the anti-depressants, I went and taught myself mindfulness and healing techniques through energy work. This went to the source of the stress and within a short period of time, my pain went away.

Always seek to understand the source, rather than just the symptom. My ex-wife's father who was a lovely man was given a pill for every ill, rather than targeting the source of his actual problem. He was given one pill for bone cancer, which then caused reflux, so he was then given another pill for the reflux, which he didn't originally have. A lot of physical ailments come or can be triggered by emotional or mental stress, and if you can work out what that is and change your way of thinking, acting, and feeling, you may just find the symptoms naturally go away over time. I truly believe most ailments, including cancer, can be caused or triggered by stress. So, based on this, if you are ever suffering with a physical ailment or some type of chronic pain, go into a state of awareness and ask yourself, "Am I following my true heart in terms of my job, or am I with the right partner in love?" What often happens is, if you are doing something that isn't aligned to your heart or your true mission in life, your body will react in a way to sometimes cause you pain, to wake you up and get you to change your life in some way or form. Or change a bad habit. Constant self-awareness checks can be a really powerful way to keep tabs on where you are in life.

If we are to take it as fact, that your body will sometimes cause you pain when you are on the wrong track, you can use this tool in decision-making in life. You can actually say to your own body, "Body, show me a feeling; in my body, that indicates the answer to the question I have is a "yes,"" then wait in a receptive, conscious manner and see what happens. I often, get the feeling of my heart filling up with a sensation of love or joy. Then, ask your body again, "Body, show me a feeling inside that indicates the answer to my question, that I am pondering, is "no?"" Again, wait in conscious silence, and hopefully, you will get another feeling. I often get a gut wrenching feeling near my belly button, which doesn't feel nice. So, once you have those two feelings known, you can use them as a gut or heart feeling to guide you; to make decisions on certain things in your life. It can save a lot of time and stress in terms of going into the wrong deal or relationship with the wrong person. Try the exercise and play around with it, you can use it for many decisions in business and in life and it may just help you.

# THE MILLIONAIRE MORNING ROUTINE TO ENERGIZE YOUR LIFE

So far, I have discussed: firstly; how to create or find purpose in your life. Secondly; how to recognize programs and flaws that don't serve you and let go of past upsets, so that your energy and mindset is cleansed, cleared, and healed; ready for a more positive pathway in terms of future based mindset. So where next? I mentioned earlier that a lot of people struggle to get out of bed to go to work in the morning, as they lack that sense of purpose and love for what they do. Having said that, even the best people who are truly inspired sometimes get tired, and that is why it is so important to develop positive habits to get yourself into the best possible state energetically every single day. This is why having an energizing morning routine to start the day can be really effective. It can set you up for the day and set the intention of getting into a positive flow state.

When I was in the investment world working in London, my morning routine started with my alarm going off at 6.15am. I would never use the snooze button. Instead, I always got up straight away, one, so I didn't wake my partner up and two, I believe in setting the intention of embracing the day with a sense of excitement and gratitude for being alive. If life is a gift and you set the intention of springing out of bed and showcase that to your own subconscious mind, then I believe the mind will create positive patterns to support you in a positive way. Focus and intentionality are key in all aspects of success in life, and by setting the intention of getting up in that positive state, you can align positive energy to your entire day.

Once up, I would make my side of the bed, because by making my side of the bed, I would automatically complete one task for the day, which would help me get into the zone for completing further tasks later on. I also had a pint of water next to my bed and would drink the whole thing in one go to rehydrate my body and stimulate the metabolic system straight away. Sometimes, I would put lemon in it, as it would make the water alkaline, which is better for your body. They say disease can only operate in an acidic body, not an alkaline one, and I know quite a few friends who have filter systems for their water that alkaline the water for you. In fact, one friend told me, he had one for years, and that his dog was eighteen years old, which is super-old for a dog. He put this all down to the alkaline water the dog was drinking. They also say that most heart attacks happen to old people in the morning, as they are dehydrated because they are afraid of drinking too much before they go to bed, as they don't want to wake up to go for a pee too many times during the night. This means it is very important to hydrate properly in the morning. Personally, I think it's better to be properly hydrated before you go to bed as well, even if you have to go to the toilet at night. In time, you develop a skill of being able to almost sleep walk to the toilet and then go straight back to sleep afterwards. The other reason for drinking water straight away, when you wake up, is to help push anything still in your digestive system along and help flush out the toxins in the body.

Next, I would look over at my partner in a state of love and gratitude and when still married with younger children, I would often pop into their rooms while they still slept and give them a gentle kiss on the cheek in gratitude and love for them. Gratitude is such a powerful tool to produce positivity, and doing it first thing in the morning is a good way to set you in the right tone of thought for the day. Gratitude produces a positive mindset and more energy. If you think about, I have two children, and if I give them a present and they are not grateful, do you think I feel like giving them anything else? Of course not! So why would the Universe, God, Allah, your own subconscious or whatever you believe in, give you anything else in the future if you are not grateful for even the smallest of things you have received or created in your life up to now. Even if you don't believe in any deity; if you show gratitude for all you have, then your subconscious helps you to open up and feel worthy enough to receive more in the future. So, be grateful for the food you eat, the house you live in, the bed you sleep in, the people you love, and the experiences you have had and watch the wonders that will come to you. The other great thing about the attitude of gratitude is that is makes you more high-vibe in terms of positivity and as we know your vibe attracts your tribe. So, the more grateful you are, the higher vibe you will be and in turn probably attract more successful people into your life. Remember, though, that complaining is the opposite of gratitude, so be aware of what you complain about and try and not complain at all. As said earlier, complaining just wastes time and energy. If something annoys you, take responsibility and take action, rather than wasting your breath complaining about. Also remember, when you point the finger, there are always three pointing back at you. So, take responsibility and act.

The next thing I would do is walk downstairs and out into the garden onto the grass. This was so that I grounded myself and woke myself up ready for the day, taking in some deep breaths of fresh air. It is such an amazing feeling to get out of bed and a few minutes later to feel the grass between your toes. The earth has a natural energy within it, as does your body, so bare feet on the soil can allow you to connect energetically with the earth, which has a very positive effect on the body.

In fact, I heard a story of a lady who had a serious ailment and she said she cured it by walking daily in the forest in her bare feet. If I woke up and it was raining, I would do a quick visualization technique to ground myself, instead of going outside. I would visualize myself as if I was an oak tree with my head and arms as the branches, leaves, and top of the tree. My stomach and chest the trunk. My legs the roots. I would then visualize energy coming down the tree through my central nervous system, out the bottom of my roots and deep down into the center of the earth, as if I or my roots were connecting with a pool of energized water at the center of the earth. I would then pull this water up my roots, up my central nervous system, and out the top of my head, then energetically visualizing a waterfall of beautiful energy coming back down into my heart. Next, I would feel the heart energy, breath in with love and then expand my energy out and visualize it as an expanded bubble of protective energy or violet light around my whole body, sealing around me in an energetic state of intention that I was bulletproof for the day. Violet is supposed to be the highest frequency of light so the intention there was to transmute lower frequency energy into a higher state, or negative energy like worry and stress into more positive energy. The protection exercise is done just in case of any people I walked past or interacted with, who were in a negative state and had lower vibrational energy. For example, they may have had an argument with their spouse and have an energy of anger still within them. So, I wanted to protect my energy so that I stayed in optimal state. Quantum physics has proven that we all have auric fields around our body (auras), and if you are standing or sitting next to someone on the train, you can sometimes feel their energy. I'm sure you have had a meeting with someone before and at the end of the meeting, you just felt drained. I found when I first started speaking on stage in front of large audiences, if I didn't do these techniques, I would be more tired coming off the stage than if I did. Surprising, I know, but true. While speaking of stages, I have proved this protection technique to work onstage at a number of my events. I have asked preferably a lady up on to the stage and asked her to hold her arm out sideways, parallel to the floor and then answer three questions. Then, using kinesiology (which is muscle testing), I would show the audience that each time she answered the question correctly, I couldn't push her arm downwards as she held her strength. I then would get the audience to send negative energy towards the woman in the form of them saying to themselves that she had bad hair or something similar. I then would go back to the lady and asked her the same three questions. This time, when I pushed down on her arm, she was not able to keep her arm up, proving that her energy had weakened and suggesting that it been affected by the people's negative thoughts towards her. After guiding the woman through the energy protection and grounding exercise, I asked the audience to resend the negative energy and asked her the three same questions again. This time, her arm remained straight and firm. It proved to the live audience that she was protected and grounded from the negative energy.

Linked to this; a top tip if you are traveling between time zones and you have the potential of jetlag is to sit on the grass at your destination, or walk in your bare feet. It really helps to ground you in to the energy of the area and reducing the jetlag.

Once grounded, I would then go back in and go and have a shower, flicking the shower onto cold three times, for a minute each time, in order to stimulate the vagus nerve and get the endorphins moving around my body. Having a cold shower also makes you step outside of your comfort zone and feel like a powerhouse or that you have already achieved something great at the start of the day. Cold showers are also supposed to be good for people with depression and stress. During my shower, I would start to visualize the day and visualize and plan what I needed to do during the day in a state of energetic intention. Top tip, though; I would highly recommend making sure you put the shower temperature gauge back to the warm position, as I have had some unfortunate, but slightly funny circumstances where my partner has gone for a shower afterwards and there has been a high-pitched scream from the shock of the cold water and a lot of disgruntled negative energy coming loudly from the bathroom. As I mentioned, it is always important to show empathy to others. Not everyone wants to do things your way, and it helps to respect that if you want a partner to stay as your partner.

Once finished in the shower, I would brush my teeth, and in the process of brushing my teeth, I would look at myself in the mirror and say to myself or out loud if possible, "I am feeling fantastic, I am having a fantastic day. I am the best businessman in my industry, I am going to make other people's day better today. I am amazing, I am brilliant, I am fantastic in all that I do." These are positive affirmations to get me motivated and ready for the day. They are also suggestive positive affirmations to help get into the best possible state mentally and emotionally. I often say to myself, "I love and approve of myself" over and over again, as long as no one is nearby of course, otherwise, you look a bit odd. I certainly don't advise talking to yourself out loud in public, as you might get a few funny looks. In all seriousness, though, people who truly like and love themselves in a non-egotistical way tend to be more confident in themselves, and confidence also tends to bring about better communication skills. This, in turn, means you will be able to work better in a team, or manage and lead people in a better way in business. Even in dating, you sometimes see these really ugly guys with these beautiful women and you wonder why, and quite often it's not money, it's confidence. Confidence brings an energy and a persona about you that people like and want to be around. So, do lots of positive self-talk, and I guarantee there will be positive effects on your life. To improve your self-confidence, you improve your self-love, and remember, love is an emotion, an energy-in-motion. Becoming more intelligent about your emotions makes you more confident about yourself, and that is why emotional intelligence is so important to work on.

Once finished in the bathroom, I would then get dressed, looking smart, and head out the door. I would walk about a mile to the train station, automatically getting some exercise and blood flow. During my walk or during any travel time, I would sometimes listen to a podcast or audiobook to learn something new or get inspired. Then, at the train station, I would say a few hellos to friends, discuss any news, and then board the train, which was a half-hour journey into the center of London. Again, this time was carefully planned. The first five minutes was finishing off the conversations I had on the platform, then the next five minutes, I would write down or type into the phone my goals and tasks for the day and double check the diary, planning ahead for what I needed to do. Then, the last twenty minutes of the train journey, I would close my eyes and meditate, visualizing getting all my tasks done, visualizing success, and also allowing my mind to relax and get ready for the day. Quite often, I would listen to some meditation music to drown out any talking or noise around me. Once off the train, I had another mile of walking, which also meant more exercise, more fresh air, and a positive state ready for the day. If I walked with a friend, we would mastermind work scenarios and how to deal with them. If I walked by myself, I would quietly say positive affirmations to myself, setting the intention of having a fantastic day and being the most successful businessman in the company. I would quite often whisper as I walked without moving my lips, "I am the best salesman in the industry, I am adding massive value to my clients, I am bringing in the most amount of business in my company," and funnily enough, it worked—try it yourself. When I arrived in the office, I would have a healthy breakfast of fruit and cereal, chatting in my office with my secretary and support staff planning the day.

So, let's summarize… I got up, made my bed, drank a pint of water, showed and thought of gratitude, grounded myself, protected my energy, had a cold shower, did some positive affirmations, dressed smartly with intention, had some exercise, then wrote some goals and tasks for the day, meditating visualizing on those goals and tasks being successful, did even more exercise, while doing some more positive affirmations, and then, ate a healthy breakfast before starting the day. I would sometimes also journal on the train if I had a lot on my mind in terms of a brain dump. You can get it out of your head and onto the paper in order to empty the worries and the ideas out, so that you can open your brain up to receive more. Also, having so much on your mind can cause a bit of stress, and that's why doing a brain dump onto paper can be very therapeutic. Journaling on a regular basis where you just write whatever comes into your mind without even thinking can also be a great way to open up the creative side of the brain. I have heard a lot of actors, speakers, and authors do this to help them in their field.

So, how long did my morning routine take? Well, it was built into my day, so it didn't take up too much of my time, at all. The kisses to the children and the gratitude was two minutes, the grounding exercise two minutes, and the affirmations while brushing my teeth maybe an extra minute. I also always shave in the shower, so that saves me time. Plus, I always have shirts ironed for the week and even have my ties already tied up to save time in terms of a quick slip on and tighten. So, what is the point of the morning routine? To optimize my energy to optimize my performance in my job and my day and to get me motivated or even inspired for the best possible day.

I also used to go for a run either between meetings, at lunchtime, or at the end of the day, although I would highly recommend just before lunch, as it will invigorate you for the afternoon, and they have proven that people in universities and schools who do exercise in the morning or before their exams tend to do better in terms of results. It makes sense; more blood flow means more clarity and quicker thinking. During the day, I was always in a constant state of awareness of time and using it to the optimum. I would arrange meetings with clients close geographically,

I studied where the best place to get on the train was in the underground to get off the other end at the right exit point, so that I wouldn't get caught behind a queue of people. I always walked up escalators, as it was an opportunity for blood flow and exercise and also optimizing time. If I was out seeing clients, I would also always put meetings geographically close together and usually schedule three meetings out of the office two either side of a lunch meeting, so that I could get into the office, prepare for the meetings, and do any administration before I left. Then when I got back in the afternoon, I could follow up on the meetings, do sales calls on the phone, or sort out managerial issues with my team.

It was all about optimizing my time and careful planning. This was all set up by the morning routine where I would get myself into the best possible flow state, the best possible energetic state to make the most of my day. One success tip I also used; was when I was early for a meeting with a large corporation, I would always go in and make friends with the receptionists and find out any knowledge there was to know about what was going on within the organization. I also found by turning up early, you could get a sense for the vibe of the organization and almost hone into the energy of the place. I also found it useful to sit in the reception in some of the bigger stockbrokers who had lots of portfolio managers who I knew. Because quite often, they would nip out for a coffee or a cigarette and they would pass me in reception, and I would get an opportunity to say hello. There was one company called Investec, for example, who I would always turn up early because I had presented so many times there and a lot of the managers knew me. So, I could turn up half an hour early to see one person and end up seeing ten others as they would pass by reception. It was a very clever use of time. Imagine, Investec had five products (funds) they bought from my company. So, if I happened to be there, shook ten hands before a meeting, I could end up getting ten deals in that day, just because of the friendships and energetic bonds I had created with these clients. In business, always aim for long-term friendships, not short-term sales. People feel that energy, and respect you so much more for that. A lot of my clients from large institutions like the Swiss bank UBS are friends on Facebook because I had built a genuine friendship and long-term relationship with them. Success in life is all down to our relationships. Good relationships mean easier and more effective communication, meaning more success with less stress.

On the way home again on the train, for the first five or ten minutes, I would either chat or read the newspaper or finalize a few bits of work and then meditate again for the last fifteen minutes, getting into a relaxed state before getting home. In my mind, I would play out certain interactions during the day and use visualizations where I could have done better or letting go of any energies that didn't serve me, so that when I got home, I would be in a relaxed and positive state. It was a time for reflection, relaxation, and reset. Once home, I would spend time with the kids if they were there, my partner, and then either go training for sport or another run. Before bed, I would meditate, do an energy clearing technique, and say positive affirmations in terms of "I am grateful" statements, which I will go into later in more detail when I talk about goalsetting.

I would highly recommend you create some kind of morning and evening routines in your life. You obviously don't have to use all of mine, but it might just give you a few ideas. Whatever it takes to get you into a great state is always good for you. Some people are naturally aligned and can go into that flow state without having to do any of these routines or habits. The ones I relayed are just a few I do to optimize the start of my day. If I was to recommend three things only, it would be gratitude statements, exercise, and meditation. Meditation is also very important, as it helps you connect to your inner self, your best self, your soul self, so that you can come from your heart space in making decisions, rather than your headspace, which can be ego (Edging God Out, which is another one of my fun acronyms for you). It is always better to make decisions in life from a place of love, rather than fear, and that is one of the things meditations can help you do. It is also great for reducing stress to increase energy for life, and finally, it can help you visualize your goals, your dreams, and your wishes, and the steps to achieve them. A billionaire friend of mine lies on his couch in his office at the start of each day and visualizes his day ahead. He visualizes his tasks to do and his goals in a state of energetic intention of celebration for achieving them all successfully by the end of the day. He also visualizes his longer terms goals as well. He swears this is the only thing he does in respect to a morning routine but also puts it down to the secret of his success in business and in life. Based on the guests on my radio show where I have interviewed around three hundred people; ninety percent of them all meditate in some way or form. It's all about energy, focus, and increasing performance to get more done, in less time, with less stress.

Whatever you find works for you is the answer. We are all different, so play around with the ideas and enjoy!

# USING ENERGY FOR CONSCIOUS CREATION THROUGH A CONSCIOUS MIND

So far, in order to charge yourself up for success in life, we firstly worked on heightening your energy levels through the discovery of your life purpose. This obviously leads to more vitality because you are doing something you love or has a real sense of meaning to it. Having purpose in your life and in your business also gives you a direction to build aligned goals around. We discussed three main ways to find your purpose. These were, one, to find what you love doing, are good at doing, and you can add value to others. Two, you link what you do to bettering someone's life, even if it's indirectly, and three, as I mentioned before, you turn your mess into a message to give it meaning and use it to help others in some way or form.

Once a sense of purpose was established, we then looked at the triggers, the traits, the traumas, and the parental programs that we may have been holding onto that don't serve us. This was to help you be able to focus on what you want, rather than what you don't want in life and create win-win with the difficult people who come into your life. Also, to help you focus on your fabulous future, rather than the problems of the past. Hopefully, through the awareness and forgiveness exercises, you have got rid of these energetic stress factors or stuck energies-in-motion, i.e. emotions within. Remember, there are always going to be some people who find it very hard to look at their imperfections, as they think they are perfect. The problem with thinking you are perfect is that you never learn anything new. A lot of people think they are special and above others, in my opinion it is much better to see yourself as adaptably average and that everyone around you has something to teach you. That way, you will automatically open yourself up to learning, growth, and also make you more interested in other people and what they have to offer. This, in turn, will make you more likable and have better relationships with other people.

Thirdly, we went through daily habits and routines to help us perform with the highest amount of energy and focus possible. And this leads us on to the next part of the puzzle, which is to set up goals that align with your purpose or mission in order to give you a direction and a clear vision of where you are and where you want to go to in life. This is the same in life as it is in business, because the leader of the business needs to align the entire organization towards the collective goal. As does a captain or coach of a sports team. This is where energy and alignment of that energy is so important. Let's face it: if you have an organization where people are positive and purposeful about where they are, what they are doing, and where they are going, you have a great groundwork to work from. If you have an organization where people are gossiping, complaining, and distracted, it isn't going to work. They often say in sport, you are only as strong as your weakest link. I believe that is true in some cases, however, if you have an exceptional leader whose energy and passion is sky high, then sometimes, those weak links can consciously rise to a higher level through the correct inspiration, communication, and engagement. That is why it is so important as a leader to be the best version of yourself and lead by example.

It is interesting that the word leadership has the word 'ship' in it, and in life, you are the captain of your ship, and you lead yourself in the direction that you want to go. As we know, a ship goes from port to port with a goal or a reason for doing so. You, as the leader of your life, need to choose goals that align with your sense of purpose, your values, and what you truly believe in. In terms of the ship, it is an interesting analogy, as the old sailing ships had sails on them, and the sailors were skilled in understanding how the energy of the wind could be harnessed in order to sail the ship as efficiently as possible in the right direction. This is the same in life. You can set out your purpose and your goals, but it is very much in your best interest to know how to harness energy in the best possible way to make your goals happen in the most efficient manner. In a love relationship, for example, if you know each other's expectations, needs, and values, you can align your energy towards them in order to make sure you are onboard the ship of life together and going in the right direction. In business, if you know the expectations, needs, and values of your customer, it is much more likely that you can provide them with a solution or product that serves them. This is where conscious communication and active listening come in.

Whether in business or life, energy is key to success. A leader, for example, uses voiced energy to communicate messages to align people to their goals and tasks, leading them towards a successful outcome for the organization. If he or she communicates in a positive, vibrant way,

i.e. high frequency, he or she can increase the vibrancy of the people they are speaking to and, in turn, inspire them to have more energy and focus towards what they are doing. We can learn to harness and use the energy within us, around us, and within the earth to create our dreams, wishes, and goals in life.

Before we get specifically into setting and achieving your goals, it is important to set the foundation and understanding of energy, itself.

Think of it this way; have you ever walked into a room where two people have just had an argument, and you can feel the tension in the room, and you just want to turn around and run straight back out? Or have you ever had a really busy week in work and you're absolutely shattered and you know you have a party you have to go to at the end of the week. Before you go, you make a pact with yourself or your partner that you will leave early. Then, you arrive at the party, and the joy, the happiness, the laughter, and the banter inspire you, and the next minute, you're dancing your socks off at two in the morning and you feel fantastic the next day. Have you ever had that? What is that? Well, it's energy, of course, both positive and negative, affecting your body based on the environment you are in and the people you are hanging around with. Hang around with a bunch of clowns and you may end up one yourself, hang around with a bunch of inspirational people and you might learn something and become an inspiration yourself.

I said at the start of the book everything in this world is made of energy; thoughts are energy, words are energy, thoughts lead to words, words lead to actions, actions lead to habits, and habits lead to destiny. So, start with a positive thought end with a positive destiny. There is energy in communication between people, and that energy can be sensed through all five senses, but also a sixth sense. A sense of intuition or gut feeling can make the difference of making the right decision, choosing the right partner, employing the right person for a job, and many other scenarios in life. If you optimize your energy, you can optimize your performance in business and in life.

Einstein once said that energy can never be created or destroyed; it just moves from one form to another. In most ways, that is true, however, in terms of spiritual and love energy, I wouldn't entirely agree.

Having been through relationship breakups where my energy was negatively affected by the emotions of sadness, I felt drained. Then suddenly I got a message from my ex-partner and my energy would shoot up from nowhere with excitement. Where did that energy come from? It didn't move from one form to another—it was created, by emotions, it was created by love. This goes back to what I said earlier that you can create energy from a sense of purpose and a sense of love for what you do, a love for the people you work with and a love for the clients you serve.

As we know, all things are made of atoms or cells. These atoms are not connected by glue; they are connected by energy, and energy has a vibration and frequency. Even a piece of lead metal has vibrating atoms within it. Inside every atom, there are electrons, protons, and neutrons moving around at light speed within empty space, all of this being pure energy. This is why if you split an atom, you can create an amazing amount of energy. This means a tree or a flower or even a piece of grass is full of energy. Vibrant energy. I realized that everything is made of energy and interconnected through energy when I was going through my near-death experience. During the experience, I was encapsulated in an amazing feeling of love, energy and connection. I felt like I was connected to everything in a state of love.

I am more spiritual than religious, but there is a part of the Bible where it says that God made man in His own image. Well, having had the near-death experience, I don't believe that is the flesh and bones of our body, I believe that is the real us, the energy within, the soul. I believe that God, Allah, Buddha, Krishna, universal energy, or whoever or whatever you believe in can be likened to the sea, and we are each a bucket of that sea. The same energy, just separated in order to experience life in a state of physicality in terms of this reality we call life. I say separated, but I believe we never are truly separated. We can tap into and connect with universal energy any time we want through intention or meditation. I am sure in the past you may have thought of an old friend who you haven't seen in a while and suddenly over the next few days, you either hear from them or bump into them in some way or form.

I actually had an extreme example of this happen to me a couple of years ago. I was out shopping with my daughter, having a Daddy-daughter day, and on the way home, she said to me, "Dad, I really love you but this energy stuff you talk about on stage, I think it's a load of rubbish."

I looked at her and smiled a knowing smile. "Okay, Sarah, let's put it to the test and see if I can prove to you that it works. Pick a friend of yours that you haven't heard from for a while and you don't expect to see?"

She replied, "Okay, Dad, let's go for Emily."

Now I know Emily, so this was a perfect choice. I immediately started to visualize Emily and Sarah in touch, and I got Sarah to do the same as well. By visualizing this, I was setting the energetic intention in my head and then getting Sarah to do it as well. Remember that thoughts are energy and energy is vibration and where focus goes, energy flows. So, by Sarah and I together energetically focusing on the same thing, we were creating a vibration or frequency collectively around what I wanted to happen in order to show her the power of energy.

Next, I said, out loud, three times to Sarah, "I am grateful to God that Emily gets in touch with you very soon." I then got Sarah to close her eyes and visualize seeing Emily, and say the "I am grateful" statements three times as well, from her perspective. Again, here I was using voiced energy to create even more intentional frequency and vibration around the energetic goal we had set.

After doing this, we drove straight back to her mother's house. Sarah got out of the car and went into the hallway of the house, while I waited at the doorway, as my son was coming over that evening to stay with me. As I was waiting, Sarah went in and saw there was a letter there for her. She opened the letter and her face dropped instantly in surprise. She looked like she'd seen a ghost. She never gets letters, and sure enough it was from Emily, hand-delivered only twenty minutes beforehand.

That was in July. Later that September, when I went to pick Sarah up from school and was waiting for her, the first person I saw at the school myself was Emily out of a school with over 500 students. That is the power of intention, the power of energy, and the power of where focus goes, energy flows.

When creating the life we want, we need to realize that everything is energy and everything has a frequency. If you want something to be brought into your energy field and your life, you need to align with that frequency or vibration of what you want in life. Think about it, talk about it, and put actions towards it. Same in a business; align people towards your collective goal or mission, and where focus goes, energy flows.

The Japanese professor Dr. Emoto's research on water focuses on the effect that the energetic thoughts, spoken words, and intentions can have on water molecules. His book, *The Hidden Messages in Water*, was a bestseller and what it revealed was astounding. Emoto took a number of water-filled containers, and on the outside, he wrote different words: for example; on one of them, there was the label of 'love,' on another one, 'hate,' and another one, 'gratitude,' and many other differently worded labels. Then, he would put each container in separate rooms with a different set of his researchers or students. Each group would then say the word on the label with meaning over and over again. So, for example, in one room, they would say to the water – "I love you, I love you, I love you," over and over again for around ten minutes. And then in another room, to another container, a different set of students would voice, "I am so grateful, I am so grateful, I am so grateful" to that water. Finally, the third group of people would voice to the container with hate on it, "I hate you" over and over again. In this way, he created an energetic resonance within the water. He then took these water containers and put them into a freezer. After a few days, he took them out and looked at the iced water molecules under a powerful microscope. He produced beautiful images to show the outcomes of what he saw, and I will briefly describe here as best I can, but, I suggest you look them up on the Internet as well. In terms of the results, the 'love' molecules were in a symmetrical, diamond-like shape, very much like you'd see in a diamond engagement ring. The same with the gratitude molecules. Whereas the 'hate' molecules were all over the place, with no pattern, and they didn't very look nice at all.

So, based on the fact that your body is made up of 65 percent water, if you are hanging around with a bunch of clowns who are talking negatively or gossiping constantly in a negative way in your company, it theoretically can actually affect your entire body in a bad way. If you think about it, if your water molecules in your body are all exposed to love and gratitude, then they will be formed into diamond-like shapes that are symmetrical and aligned together. This will allow a better flow of energy through your body, and in turn, you will think and react better, thus helping you perform better.

We can easily feel negativity effecting the body, too. I am sure you may have a had a meeting with a negative client before, or had a date with a negative person and came away from the experience feeling drained. This is why it is so important to protect and ground your energy to prevent this happening, the same way I described earlier. It is also why it is so important to make sure the thoughts you have about yourself are positive, so the self-talk in your head is positive. Let's face it: you are the person who talks to yourself the most. Sometimes, it can be the most intelligent conversation you have, so you might as well make it positive as well. It is proven that positive self-talk is good for your mental, emotional, and even physical wellbeing, as we can see from Dr. Emoto's experiments.

So, often, whether in business or in life, we find negative faults in ourselves and others; no wonder there are problems in terms of mental wellness in the world. Look for the positives in people, look for the positives in yourself, and you will improve your relationships, your teamwork skills, and your performance in life.

What is also worth considering is that there is water all around us. For example, there are water pipes, central heating systems, and drainage systems. Water is also in our food, and the drinks we consume. In fact, I believe it is potentially beneficial to voice positive words out loud while you are cooking over and over again to create positive water molecules in the food you are about to consume, so that it is better for your body. I also think it could be the reason why a lot of people have cured themselves of ailments, by going vegan and organic. There is a love that is put into growing the food, whereas I wonder how much love a cow feels when it is lining up to be butchered. One might say the cow can't tell what is about to happen to it, but my question is based on sixth sense, is it able to feel energy? Who knows? And have you ever been to a slaughterhouse and felt the energy? I actually have the word love written on all the undersides of all of my furniture; chairs, tables, cupboards, beds, everywhere, because based on Dr. Emoto's experiments, you just never know.

My mother has little red love hearts on every door of the inside of her house to create the intention of love. I have to say everyone comments on how lovely the energy is in my house and in my parent's house. On the flip side, you can also feel an eerie energy in a funeral home or in a graveyard or even in a house where someone has been murdered in the past. Dr. Emoto's experiments prove that thoughts, intention, and voiced energy have a vibration, and that vibration can affect everything around. So, use your energy wisely to create positivity around you, in your relationships, and in your place of work.

When I was a kid, I was always told that, "Sticks and stones may break your bones, but words can never hurt you." Well, I'm not so sure about that now. The power of the word can create both positivity and negativity for you and others around you. So, use your words very wisely, because your word is your wand. I also believe that everything that you voice has a resonance and frequency. In fact, isn't it amazing that you can be on the phone talking to someone on the other side of the world and the sound they hear is exactly the same as if you were in the same room? The voiced energy comes out of your mouth vibrating onto the atoms in the air to create the sound of what you said, it then goes into the receiver of the cellphone and up to the satellite as a wave of energy. It then comes back down into the phone of the person at the other end and then converted back into sound energy, which vibrates in the air into the ear, allowing the other person to hear what you have just said. Now, thinking about it, there are eight billion people on this planet and apparently around five billion phones, so that can mean that there are millions of people speaking on phones and Zoom calls all over the world at any time.

This means there is energy in the atmosphere all around us, and if energy never dissipates, it can mean that there is the possibility that every single idea and every spoken word is still in the earth's atmosphere in an energy wave, and anyone can potentially tap into these spoken words and even potentially thought patterns if they are aligned to that frequency.

It's a bit like when I would go skiing in France; when I was younger, I was pretty fluent in French, and if I go into a French bar and actually tune into the words around me, I can pick up the words and understand. If I don't tune in, I just hear blah, blah, blah in the background, and it can sound meaningless. That is the same with the energy field around us or the collective consciousness, as it's often called; I believe this is like a storage area for the energetic words that have been voiced in the past. If you adjust your frequency like a radio dial, these energies can be honed into through tools like meditation.

If done correctly, it is amazing what insights can come into your head. I also believe that people who are psychic can hone into this more easily. This is also the reason they can read people's minds, because there is an energetic resonance of the past things that the person has said and thought, still in their auric or energetic field around their body, and a sensitive psychic can pick up on these.

There is another side to this, which I think is important to consider. If you are able to, one, pick up on other people's thoughts and two on the resonance from past voiced or thought energy; then you need to be able to differentiate the difference between your own thoughts, that are actually part of you, and thoughts that you might be picking up on from outside of you. As an example of what I mean, let's say you and your spouse have an argument about how to parent a naughty child. One might say the child should be put in the naughty corner, the other might say just a quick telling off will do and leave it at that. This kind of argument is very popular, and when you get into that resonance of that thought pattern; in terms of what the right answer is, you may attract previous people's voiced energy vibration on what they thought or said as a solution. Some could be negative, and some could be positive. People always talk about having an angel and a devil giving them different opinions on things they think about. Well, maybe it is just that they are tapping into negative or positive thought patterns that already exist in the atmosphere, and this is why it is important to take your emotions out of any decision-making in a state of awareness and make the decision based from love and from your heart, rather than from fear and potentially negative ego. It could also explain when people have said, "The answer came to me out of nowhere."

I do wonder if some people who are highly sensitive to energy can get affected by certain energies to the extent that it makes them feel not themselves. This might seem a bit out there, but perhaps they are being affected by external energy waves and it makes them think and act in a different way than normal. If you are hungover, which is an imbalance of chemical energy, you can act grumpy. It you are too hot in the sun, you can act with a short temper because of heat energy and become hot and bothered. We can sense the energy of someone, who is in a bad mood, without them even speaking; so why could it not be feasible that someone, who is highly sensitive to energy, is being affected in a way by the energy waves around them? I was at a concert one time and the loud music gave one of my friends a headache and he became grumpy. He normally is one of the most positive people I know. Vibrational energy is all around us, and with the introduction of mobile phones, it is even more so. Perhaps, this is why there seems to be an increase of people having problems with attention span—they are tapping into the energy waves and getting distracted.

Let's take an extreme example like a battlefield in war; there is violence, anger, fear, screams, and shouts of negative energy all over the battlefield. Based on what Einstein said, energy never dissipates, it just moves from one form to another, perhaps all this negative energy can bind together in a state of consciousness to form a larger negative energy form, then, if it comes into contact with someone who is resonating at a lower frequency because they are depressed, or have an ailment, then maybe there is the possibility, that the negative energy form can affect that person in a detrimental way. Or, perhaps another way you could look at it, is that all negative energy forms can be likened to stuck negative emotions, like we discussed earlier in the book, and with right intention, they can be energized back into higher frequency energy, which is more positive. This can be done through interaction with high vibration energy or by the use of energetic techniques used by some practitioners like myself. Certain people like myself can tap into positive energy in the atmosphere or from a higher frequency field and channel that energy into the person who is suffering. In turn being able to create a higher vibration within the person they are treating and allowing them to release the negative energy naturally. Or, transmuting whatever energy that was attached to them, that was disrupting their energy field, back up to a higher frequency field in the atmosphere. That's why it is important to do the grounding and energy protection techniques I mentioned earlier, as you can stop this happening in the first place. Having said that some people resonate at such a high level that they just transmute all negative energy forms around them back into higher frequency. Also, quantum physics has proven that we all have an auric field around us. I believe this is a bit like the ozone layer around the earth; it is to protect our body from energies that do not serve us and act as a filter. It is interesting that quite often, people who have had serious accidents or near-death experiences have sometimes had a change in personality after the accident. Perhaps that is because their energy field was affected in some way or form.

These ideas all come from experiences I have had personally and from clients' feedback.

I found it interesting when writing this book, as my best time for writing seemed to be from midnight to four in the morning. I wonder if it because everyone who lives in my area is asleep, so there is less voiced energy and thought waves to pick up on, meaning it is easier to focus on my own self? Who knows?

In terms of high-performance or charging yourself up for success, why am I telling you all this? It sounds a bit out there in terms of concepts and how can it help you? Well, I believe it is important to manage your physical body in terms of wellbeing, your emotional body in terms of your emotions, your mental body in terms of your thoughts, and your spiritual body in terms of your energy within. In turn you will optimize your thoughts, your behaviors, your habits, and your feelings to create win-win in all the interactions you have in life, including the interactions with your own self. My viewpoint is the most grounded version of consciousness is self-awareness, which is part of emotional intelligence. I also believe that the thoughts we have and the words we speak are both made up of energy, so, by understanding this, you can use this knowledge of energy to create your goals in a much better way

It's incredible; how much the energy of our thoughts and the energy of our words can affect us and the people around us. This is why we need to be very conscious of the thoughts we have, the words we say, and the actions we take. It is important to voice what you want, rather than what you don't want. For example, when people around me first started to realize that I was able to help people in terms of healing and also through the manifestation of what I say; they would ask me; "It's my wedding day next month, can you pray, visualize or affirm, that it's not going to rain on my wedding day?" And I always said no, because in that sentence, you've got the words 'rain' and 'wedding day' together, and that could potentially create what you don't want. Instead, what I would do; is pray or say affirmations for the fact that there's going to be blue sky and sunshine, only, on their wedding day, in order to create what they wanted and not what they didn't.

In terms of this, I used to often say to people that this situation or that person was a pain in the ass. It was one of the most common phrases I used, back when I was younger. My father also used to say the same thing to me when I was a kid, if I was bragging about how wonderful I was to try and get his attention. Well, as I have said already, 'your word is your wand' and sometimes 'the sentences we say can be the sentences we condemn ourselves and others too'… I ended up actually getting a pain in the ass and had to have two operations there in 2009, which did not go well. This then led to three years of chronic pain until I had my near-death experience. It was very unpleasant and led to me suffering from massive stress, anxiety, and depression. Thankfully, I am now in perfect health. I believe you have to be so careful about the words that you use. In fact, another thing both my father and I would voice regularly was; "this is a pain in the back" or he might say to me "you are a pain in the back", and sure enough, at age eighteen, I was playing rugby and I got an injury where I cracked my vertebra slightly and had a pain in the back. Later in my thirties, I used the words 'pain in the neck' a lot, and I ended up having a collision with someone while playing hockey and hurt my neck. My mother, also used to often say to me, "Douglas, make sure you put a coat on, otherwise you might catch pneumonia." Well, at seventeen, surprise, surprise, I caught pneumonia. No blame towards either parents. The point of these stories is to showcase how you need to be very careful about the voiced energy around you. Thankfully, at 48, I am fit and healthy, regularly running ten kilometers a day and living with my partner who is twelve years younger than me.

In terms of a few more stories I have where it showcases 'Your word is your wand' and that you can create through voiced energy, check out the below:

When I was first separated from my ex-wife, I kept my wedding ring on in front of the kids, just so I didn't upset them. It was only a couple of months since they had found out, and I didn't want to seem insensitive by taking it off too early. I then started dating, and would switch the ring onto the middle finger, so that my date would feel comfortable. There was one particular date I went on where I had forgotten to put the ring back on the middle finger, and it was still on the wedding finger. My date picked up on it and asked whether I was still married, and I was so embarrassed. I said to her, "I wish I could move it onto my middle finger permanently and my kids would be happy with it."

The next day was a Saturday, and I had the kids for that day. It was a little cold out, and I wanted to convince the kids to come to the park to get some fresh air. They were tired and not overly keen on the idea. I said to them, "Let's go to the park and have a treasure hunt." At the time, I had no idea why I said that. We had never had a treasure hunt before; it just came to me out of nowhere. So, we arrived down in the park on a cold winter's day. The leaves had fallen, and there was a golden-brown carpet all over the ground. The air was fresh and moist, and there was a definite icy feel in the air. My son and I began playing a game in the playground where we would throw the football at each other with the aim of hitting the other person with the ball, to score a point. The idea was to dodge the ball while not in possession. After five minutes of playing in the cold, my wedding ring came flying off my finger and landed on the ground in the playground amongst a floor of golden wood chippings. The next minute, my son, my daughter, and I were all having a treasure hunt for the ring. We couldn't find it anywhere. Suddenly, at almost the exact same time my ex-wife rang to say she was in the park and could she come and say hello to the kids. I agreed but told her we were looking for my ring.

The minute she arrived, I suddenly saw my ring. It was almost right in front of me; I had no idea why I hadn't seen it before. At that point, I picked it up and was about to put it back on my wedding finger when my ex said in front of the kids, "Look, you've obviously lost weight and we are separated now, so you might as well put it on your middle finger." The kids were there; they were happy, and so was I.

The night before, I had voiced my wish that I could have it on that finger, that morning I had spoken about having a treasure hunt, and we had the treasure hunt to find the ring and now I had the permission of my children's mother to permanently move the wedding ring to my middle finger. I have learned, and encourage you, to be careful about what comes out of your mouth. Good and bad.

Interestingly, three months later, I was dating a different girl who said she wished I could completely take the ring off. I said I wished I could too, and was only leaving it on for the kids. The next day, I went to pick my kids up from their mother's and saw my ex had taken her ring off. After a quick discussion with the kids to make sure they were comfortable, I took that ring off for good. I went out with that particular girl for a short while. She was lovely, but hadn't got over her ex-husband, and I suspected she was still in love with him. I really liked her, but I wanted someone who had let go of their past love for their past partner, and I asked the Universe for someone very similar, but someone who didn't have an ex-husband that they were still in love with. This girl was from Lisbon, sexy and spiritual. Within a few weeks, my ex-fiancée came into my life. She was also from Lisbon, sexy and spiritual, just no ex-husband. I thought about it, voiced it, and received it.

Roll on a year, and I proposed to my ex-fiancée. I went out and bought her a lovely ring. However, my ex-fiancée had a gold signet ring which she had inherited from her grandmother on her middle finger, next to where my ring would go. I was a little conscious that my ring wouldn't look as good next to her beautiful signet ring. I relayed this, over the phone to my mum saying, "I wish she didn't have that ring there, so that my engagement ring would look uniquely special." It was said from the heart out of love and the next day, my ex-fiancée woke up with a rash under her signet ring, and it was so itchy that she had to take it off. She was astounded, as that had never happened before and she couldn't understand it. I was almost pinching myself to stop myself from smiling so much. Nine hours later, I was down on one knee, proposing and putting the ring on her finger.

Interestingly, a few months later, she was having an interaction with my daughter, who was only eleven at the time. My daughter had told her that she felt that my fiancée was one of the reasons that her mum and dad had split in terms of marriage. This wasn't true, as I hadn't met her until six months after the marriage split, but my fiancée got upset and defensive. I felt as the adult, she was wrong for something she said, and I asked the Universe for a sign. Within less than half an hour, my now ex-fiancée got a rash underneath her engagement ring and she had to take it off. She is a wonderful girl in so many ways, but it wasn't easy for her with me having an ex-wife, who I was still friendly with and two children. My ex-wife is happily living with a lovely guy who is great to my kids, and I am very grateful for him, and I am very grateful for my ex-wife being happy. I also hope my ex-fiancée has found happiness within and a wonderful person to love her, as she deserves it. When you don't have kids and you are dating someone who has kids, I know it can be difficult, but just remember there is an unconditional love for a child that no one can understand until you have one. As a parent, we always run after our children when they are young. We will always support them, and we will always love them. As for my two children, I love them with all of my heart and love every moment I spend with them.

Family and relationship harmony are so important in terms of being able to perform in all areas of your life. They always say, "happy wife, happy life," but it goes both ways. If you feel loved, supported, and safe, then you will be able to focus better in your workplace.

I am now almost two years into another relationship with another lovely woman inside and out. Again, I met her through energetic intention. I first interacted with her on Facebook (facebook is now Meta, which if you are reading this book years from when I wrote it, Meta is one of the top social media sites in history – note by writing this and you reading this, I am setting the energetic intention that this book is going to be read for hundreds of years to come, I am creating while I write!). I met my current girlfriend on facebook the month after the breakdown of my marriage—interestingly, on the eleventh day of the eleventh month of that year. It was a just a message saying thank you, as she liked my company page. We didn't interact again for another three years, until I said to myself one day, I really could do with a massage and a healing. I had been doing a lot of coaching and healing work myself with a lot of people with depression or stress problems in work. Sometimes, even the healer needs a healing. Similarly, sometimes a CEO needs a coach, not because the coach is better than them, just because the coach can sometimes help mastermind them up to another level. Let's face it, every top sports professional has a coach, because they want to be the best, so why wouldn't you. That day I wanted help, and reached out for it. I went onto Facebook and despite having over four-and-a-half thousand friends at that time, she popped up as the first person on my Facebook feed, advertising her massage therapy. A week later, we met. A few months later, she was single, and became partners and we now live together.

There's another true story about a girl in my life that shows the power of intention and energy. The story will give you an insight into the potential of what you can create through energy in your own life. When I was eight years of age, I had a girlfriend named Claire. I used to chase her around the playground and try to kiss her all the time. She was my first girlfriend, and I was massively in love with her. One evening, my father announced that he'd taken a job over in the U.K. and that we were going to be moving away from Dublin to London. I was devastated. Not because of my friends, my home, or Ireland. It was more about the fact that I was going to be leaving this girl, Claire.

I prayed, and I kept saying, "I am sure I'm going to see her again. I'm sure I'm going to see her again." We moved again to Belgium when I was 15 and going into the very same class, at the same time, on the very first day of my new school was Claire. By then, she was a little taller than me, and we didn't work out romantically. Still, it was great to see her, and actually at one stage, I had a photo of her and my ex-wife either side of me at a party. At the time, I thought I was standing next to my first and last girlfriends. Not the case though, and interestingly, my current girlfriend looks a little bit like Claire in some ways. On top of it all my current girlfriend lived a stone's throw away from where I lived as a child, it's funny how energy works. I believe that I created the situation with Claire through love and emotion. When you visualize, pray, say positive affirmations, and truly come from your heart space, rather than just the head space, you can create anything in life. Obviously, a bit of focused action helps along the way.

Another story I heard about how successful people are very conscious of the words they use and the thoughts they have comes from Bill Gates. Bill is the founder of Microsoft, and one of the richest and wisest men in the world at the current time. There was a great documentary film on Netflix called Inside Bill's Brain. Bill is superb in it, and I thoroughly recommend you watch it. At one point, he is interviewed and is asked what his biggest fear is. He replied really wisely by saying that 'he didn't want his brain to stop working'. Now, a lot of people might say in terms of fear, in respect to that, that they didn't want to lose it in old age by getting something like Alzheimer's, Parkinson's, or dementia. However, Bill is very conscious and wise about his words and didn't want to put energy towards any of those ailments. Instead, he just said that he wanted his brain not to stop working, and in his sentence, he answers with the words "brain" and "working". So energetically, he is creating that his brain will always work perfectly, and I am very grateful that it always will. The reason I believe this to be true, is I believe the subconscious mind does not register the words 'not' and the 'hope not' in the sentences we say.

Linked to Bill Gates's story, it is interesting that I have had a lot of clients come to me and say their mother or father had dementia or Alzheimer's and after careful questioning about their language skills and how their families used to talk to their parents, I would find out that they would often use language when speaking to their parent, such as, "You're out of your mind" or "you are away with the fairies" or " you're off your head" or "you're going mad." Or the person, themselves, who got the dementia or Alzheimer's used to use the phrase that they "couldn't remember" over and over again. Said enough times, the energy behind the words can create, and it did.

There are many people who are master creators in business and life, who are powerful in terms of their words. Some are very conscious of it and others are not even aware of it. This can lead, without meaning to sabotaging themselves through the words they use. For example, we all know Donald Trump has been an incredibly successful businessman, however, there was one point where he did go bankrupt and lost all his money. Maybe he was about to make a big deal or something like that, and I wonder if someone close to him said in his presence something like, "Mr. Trump, I hope you don't lose it all in this deal," and then, he did. Luckily, though, as a master at manifesting, he knew how to recreate wealth, and sure enough, in a very short space of time, he was back up to billionaire status.

Interestingly, Donald Trump in his presidential election campaign was promoting excessively on social media leading up to the elections. He was targeting the masses on social media, rather than using old media, such as television and tours, like his competitors. I would say the very fact that people were wording and speaking so much about Trump going for president on social media, is possibly why he was successful, because where focus goes, energy flows, and my word, was there a lot of focus on Trump, both good and bad. Whether good or bad, it didn't matter; he was mentioned so much in the same sentence as the word president, that hey presto, he got it. This was the similar with Brexit in the U.K. No one really wanted it, but it was talked about so much that the thing happened.

I have witnessed people create miracles through the power of voiced energy or words and also completely sabotage themselves as well through their unconscious misuse. So, remember to think smart, talk smart, and act smart, and you will create a smart outcome for you and the people around you. In terms of the people around you, if have ambitious goals that seem like far-fetched dreams to others; you may hear them say, "Oh, you'll never do that," their voiced energy can affect you, so try and ignore and distance yourself from the naysayers and find friends and colleagues who share your vision and see your potential. This way you can stay focused and in an absolute positivity in terms of goal achievement. They do always say you are the average of the five people you hang around with, and I agree with that to an extent, especially in a business and a love relationship. Having said that, people like Gandhi, Jesus, Nelson Mandela, and Martin Luther King Jr. came from backgrounds certainly not of privilege, but became leaders who stepped into their own inner power, and made a massive positive impact on the world forever more.

So, regardless of the family you have or the background you come from, don't let it hold you back. You have the power to achieve anything in your life you want. Just connect to your inner power, your heart, and follow your dreams without limitations. You can do it—I know you can!

# EFFECTIVE GOALSETTING AND ACTION PLANNING IN LIFE & BUSINESS

There are many books written about goalsetting and how to bring your goals to life. My aim is to bring another perspective in, to make it more fun and add spiritual and energetic techniques to help you create your goals more easily. As mentioned earlier, goalsetting in life is paramount, and I am sure it is no coincidence that my near-death experience happened just after I had completed all my goals that I had set when I first left university. I was a millionaire on paper, I had a family with two kids, I owned two properties with no mortgage, I had a few hundred thousand in the bank, I had played hockey with the best players in the world, and I had been recognized in my industry as a successful businessman. All of these goals had been completed, and suddenly, I had not set any new goal, new direction, or new mission. Was it that I had done all my goals, had no more set up, and my subconscious thought, *Well, that's it then, time to go?* Or was it my soul trying to wake me up to start setting goals aligned to my true purpose, rather than my ego? Who knows? I do know that it was largely stress-related and then a virus. It certainly changed my life, making me invent a few new goals pretty rapidly—one of them, being, to get back into perfect health again. It is interesting, in my own experience of the people I have known, quite often in the past, some men who have worked till they are 65 suddenly retired and then in a short space of time, they passed away because they had no goals set for the future, and nothing to live for in life. This is why it is so important to continuously set new goals for yourself, so that you have a map and a direction for where your life is to go, even if you just remember that life is about the journey of learning more than just the destination. My goals in the past were all about ego, competition, and money, and they were not aligned to my true purpose in life. My new goals are about service to others, growing towards being the best version of myself, and continuous learning, so that I can self-improve every day, and to use my experiences and knowledge to inspire and support others on their path, too. My main purpose now and of this book is to help people connect to their true self, their best self, in order to complete whatever their true mission is in life and to help them optimize their energy in all the areas of life. If you don't have goals that are aligned to the service of others, have a think and ask yourself, *Why am I here on the planet? What am I good at? What can I add value to people in some way? or How can I help the planet, itself?*

In the following chapters I will cover my own personal experience and the experience of others in terms of successful goalsetting and achievement in business and in life. Business goals are important, as are life goals, such as manifesting a partner into your life or setting goals to get yourself into the best possible state of health, or even goalsetting for success in sport. There are so many types of goals you can set in life; think about all the areas of your life, and write down some goals that align to your heart, remember success is different for everyone.

In life, I believe service to others is key for a sense of true fulfillment, however, we all still need to make money to live and pay the bills. The COVID virus pandemic and the rise of Internet communication, has led many people to start side-line businesses to create more income. So, these business sections of the book may give you a few ideas if you are in a large organization or want to start a business to get some extra income on the side. Let's face it: we all have some knowledge or experience that we can use to help other people with, and if we put the idea into a course or a video format, there is the possibility of turning that knowledge and experience into a passive income stream, almost like a book on the side. For example, I know a brilliant mum who developed a course on conscious parenting for other parents, and she became a millionaire through her courses. If you can do something that you love talking about and adds value to people, you will definitely find yourself creating success without much stress. It would almost be like doing your hobby and making money out of it.

In order to create the life you want, it is important to understand where you are and where you want to go, and to plan with aligned goals in that direction to make it happen.

One of the most important factors in goalsetting for a business is firstly to put a business plan in place. Most company business plans are written, shown to the boss, and then put in a drawer until bonus time at the end of the year, to see how well you have done in comparison to the goals that were set. What a waste of time. It is much better to put a business plan in place with targets; not just for the year, but for the quarters, the months, even the weeks. Then put daily processes, procedures, and systems in place that help lead you towards your targets and goals. Then, visualize those tasks and long-term goals in your mind every day. It is also so important for your goals, mission, or purpose to be approached with massive, focused action, enthusiasm, and positivity. Visualize them in a sense of celebration as well, as if you have succeeded in already completing them. In fact, get yourself into the feeling and energy as if you have already achieved them, then you will feel worthy to receive them. If you do this as a group, collectively visualizing it can be very powerful, as where focus goes, energy flows. Your business plan should be like a workbook, a moving part, and it should be fun. Add in a vision board with photos of clients and people celebrating deals. Talk about it on a regular basis, create energy around it, in order to get everyone on board and interested. Whenever I got a sniff of a large potential deal from a client, I would tell my boss, the fund managers, the support team, anyone who would listen. I would do this to create an energy around the deal. The more people talking about it in our organization, the more focusing on the frequency and energy of the client, the money, and the deal. This is the same in life.

I actually think it would be massively useful if organizations got their staff all together to regularly visualize their goals and missions being completed in a meditative state. People could also put a one-page business plan on their desk or next to them on a wall, so that it can be seen by them and others. Who knows? Someone from another department could be walking by and see you have a goal to get a company like Google as a client, and the passer-by may have a friend or a family member who works there and could help you. Actually, on this point, I have been discussing with a manufacturing company about the production of small, mini white boards that can either be stuck on the wall next to you in the office or even be mounted on top of your computer. On this board, I think it would be a great idea to write down your personal goals for the week. Let's say, for example, you were training for a marathon. You might write, "Goal for the week: To do ten kilometer runs every day to train for my marathon." This way, a colleague might walk by and say, "Wow! You are doing a marathon, so am I. Would you like to train together?" What a great way to create connection through common interests within the workplace and in turn, make the workplace a more friendly and collaborative environment. By doing this, people will feel like they are coming into the office to see their friends; and as I showed earlier at the start of the book, happier staff and more positive people can affect the entire revenue of the company. Also, a more friendly environment with positive energy would mean less confrontation or quicker solutions to a difference of opinion. Let's face it: in some organizations, you can get many different people wanting their way and their opinions to be followed, and this can sometimes lead to time wasted in debates of whose idea is the best.

The word leadership has the word "ship" in it, and a ship travels in a direction, so make sure everyone is on board the ship and travelling in the same direction. Olden day ships had lots of big sails harnessing the energy of the wind to get the ship going in the right direction as quickly as possible. You could use the analogy that the leader of a business needs to use lots of salesmanship (sales) or communication skills to get everyone aligned energetically to where the organization needs to be heading. This is why it is so important to align your company mission statement, business plan and goals to a sense of purpose in terms of adding value to others in some way or form, or helping the planet. It inspires people to have more energy towards the tasks they are doing on a daily basis and creates a sense of comradery within the business. As mentioned before when I joined all of the large multinationals I worked for, I was told the mission statement on my joining day and then at the annual conference. This is just not enough; we need to be reminding our staff every single day. It needs to be on the wall behind reception, so we know the mission statement when we walk through the doors every day, and so our clients do too. It also needs to be on your website and maybe even on the back of your business card if there is space. Having your why in your psyche every day can drive passion, purpose and increase your energy for what you do.

There was a friend of mine who worked at UBS Bank, who went on to set up a business called Vestra Wealth. Ten people from UBS joined him to set the business up. He brought these ten people to work in a massive office, that would hold 150 staff. I thought it was brave, and when I met with him, I asked him why had he rented such a large office. He said to me, "Doug, I am setting a goal and business plan with the intention of what I want, not what I don't want. I am setting the intention of growth, and I want the other ten guys within the organization to see that every day. I want to enthuse them to dream big, to grow, and see the vision of where we're looking to go to in the future. Plus, to keep them on their toes in terms of the effort and focus we need to get there." Within three years, they went on to fill that office, and within five years, they had over seven billion dollars under management, and they got bought out by LGT to form LGT Vestra. This incredible performance, came about, thanks to a clear business plan with aligned goals, a vision, and a true sense of purpose. Then, effectively communicating and sharing that purpose and vision with their staff to implement connection and collaboration towards that collective goal. This CEO had a positive growth mindset, he took an action step of dreaming big, he shared the knowledge of his vision with his team, and he put a lot of energy in, to MAKE it happen.

His vision created jobs and wealth for hundreds of people, plus their products and services were excellent, so they added a lot of value to their customers. So, his goal wasn't just about him; it was about a much larger group of people, bettering their lives in a positive way. These ideals are what is needed in all goalsetting in life and business; the right mindset, focused actions, effective knowledge, and lots of vibrant energy put towards the goal, mission, dream, or purpose to MAKE it happen. It's amazing when the business plan and focus is all about adding value to others; there is more positive energy flow within the business leading, to more positive outcomes.

This last point is key in terms of making sure your goals are about adding value to others and to humanity. By doing this, it gives you much higher energy levels, as it means you are trying to positively affect others, rather than just selfishly gaining for yourself. A good example of where I witnessed how this works was when I had John Mattone on my radio show. John used to be Steve Jobs's executive coach, and in case you are reading this book in a few hundred years' time… Steve Jobs was CEO of Apple PLC, probably the most successful technology company in the world at the time of writing this book. So, John, around twenty years ago, wrote a book on leadership and sales. He wrote the book with the energetic intention of selling a load of books and getting on stages all around the world; being paid for motivational speaking. The outcome of his intention was that he didn't sell a book. Ten years later, he re-read his book and said to himself, "You know what? I know this book could help a young up and coming executive or business person be more successful and have a better life." So, this time, he re-launched the book with a different cover and the energetic intention of putting it out there just to help people in some way or form. The book became a New York Times bestseller, Steve Jobs read the book, Steve Jobs got John into his business and made him his executive coach, and then John became famous motivating people on stages all over the world. I had the pleasure of meeting him in Ireland and had him on my radio show. So, what this shows is either the Universe or your own subconscious energetically helps you much more in your goals and wishes when you make them about adding value to others, rather than just for gain for yourself.

The other lesson that we learn from the story with the UBS guys going to Vestra is to dream big and set big goals. They may seem daunting at times, but if you break the goals down into smaller goals with smaller baby steps, it can really help. Liam Ryan, who had a horrific brain tumor and was on my radio show, said to me that he had set a goal to get back into full health again after his operation. He told me at the time he couldn't even walk after his operation and treatment. The goal looked daunting, until he broke it down into smaller steps and celebrating those little steps along the way. As I mentioned earlier, when you show gratitude and celebration for the little things, the Universe or your own subconscious opens you up to receive more. Liam also told me that when he was diagnosed, he was told he had a month to live and that if he did the operation to take the tumor out, he would probably die. He told me once he had come to terms with this, he let go of the fear of death and had a real sense of gratitude for the 40 years he had been on the planet. True gratitude and no fear. These are two of the key elements of success in any goal, and I am sure it was the reason for the success of his operation and 20 years on, he is full of positive energy and inspiring people all around the world with his story. He has even since completed a marathon.

Sometimes, the greatest blockage of us achieving our goals is fear, which as an acronym is well-known as False, Evidence, Appearing, Real. What I mean by this, is fear; is an imagined future that hasn't even happened yet. So why not Face Everything And Rise to the challenge, instead.

# MINDSET, ACTIONS, KNOWLEDGE, ENERGY: "MAKE" BUSINESS THROUGH CLIENT MAPPING

The next part of business action planning is to implement is client mapping, making sure you are spending the right time with the right customers to bring in the most amount of revenue. This is where good knowledge and research can come in. It also can come down to being in the right place at the right time with the right people.

I heard a fun story to emphasize this point. There was a young man who was walking down the coast of Galway in Ireland. He looked over a cliff edge and saw these three amazing stones, gleaming like diamonds. He climbed down and picked the stones up, and when he got back home, he showed his dad;

He said to his Dad, "Dad, look at these stones. They're incredible, aren't they?"

And his Dad replied: "Wow, son, they are incredible. Do you know what you should do? You should take the first stone, go down to the local market, make a market stall, make it look pretty, then put the stone there, and if someone comes up and wants to buy it, just show them the peace sign with two fingers in the air and say nothing else."

The son created a stall and put the stone in the middle, and waited for a customer to come along. This lovely lady approached the stall seeing the stone and said, "Wow, what a beautiful stone. How much do you want for it?" The boy said nothing he just showed the peace sign with two fingers in the air. The lady replied, saying, "Two euros, wow that's a great deal, thank you very much." And off she went as happy as you like.

The boy was also pleased, and he went back to his father and said, "Dad, I got two euros for that stone. It's incredible. What will I do with the next one?"

His dad said, "Take the next stone, son, to the local diamond merchant. He sells precious stones, and see if he wants to buy it, and if he asks how much; again, just show him the peace sign with two fingers in the air and say nothing else."

The boy runs off to the diamond merchant and shows him the stone. The diamond merchant likes the stone and says, "Wow what a beautiful stone how much do you want for it?" Again, the boy doesn't say anything. He just shows the two fingers peace sign. "200 Euros?" says the diamond merchant… "Hmmm… deal, done, thank you very much," and he hands over the money.

The boy again goes back to his Dad in excitement and says, "Dad, Dad! I got €200 for that stone; that's incredible. What will I do with the last one?"

The father thinks for a minute and then says, "I'll tell you what son, take the last stone and go up to Dublin, go to the National History Museum, go into the precious stone section, find the professor, and show him the stone. If he wants to buy it, show him the peace sign and see what happens."

The boy goes up to Dublin, goes to the national history museum, goes into the precious stone department, and finds the Professor and shows him the stone. The professor says, "Wow, what a beautiful stone, I would love that for the museum collection, how much do you want for it?" The boy shows him the peace sign with the two fingers, and the professor says, "€2,000… hmmm… deal done. Thank you very much." And he hands over the money.

The boy is absolutely ecstatic and goes back to his dad in excitement; "Dad, Dad! I got €2,000 for the last stone, that's absolutely incredible. What does this mean?" And the father replied "Don't you know, son? If you value what you have to offer and hang around with the right people, you get very different results."

So, make sure that you value what you have to offer, whether it's a product, a service, or even just what's inside of you, and hang around with the right people, and you can get very different results. I found that when I was in the investment management industry, with the same product and the same presentation, I would go and see a financial advisor, and I might get £1 million. I would go and see a stockbroker, and I might get £5 million. I would go and see an asset manager, and I would get £10 million, a global bank, £100 million, and one institutional pension fund manager gave me £285 million in one deal.

Based on this premise, if I am ever going into my local town or city, instead of going to the local mainstream coffee shop, I would go to the best hotel in town and have a coffee there, instead. I'd pay the extra five euros or ten euros it might cost, because you never know who you might bump into, and personally, I have bumped into politicians, multimillionaire businessmen, and sports stars doing exactly that. Who knows? If you engage with them in a positive way, you could meet your next best friend or your next potential client that could change your life. I also encourage people, if you are flying somewhere on an airplane, to go business class or first class, if you can afford it. I don't do it to be flash or because I am tall; I do it because, again, you can actually end up sitting next to someone who could change your life for the better. I was traveling business class a few years ago, and I sat next to the CEO of Game on Media, a tech company. As we got chatting, it became clear that we could add value to one another, and he paid me several thousand euros to come into his company and deliver a keynote speech to rally the troops. So, make sure you hang around with the right people. Then, value what you have to offer, whether it be in relationships, in business, or in life.

Client mapping is key to optimizing your time and your energy, targeting your efforts in order to bring in the most amount of revenue for the least amount of work.

The principles of success, I have been talking about, are highlighted below in a real life example client of mine. The point of the case study and story is not to tell you what a great deal I made, but instead, to show you a little of the psychology behind the work to make the deal happen. When you have a large, targeted client, it is so important to look after them and treat them in the best possible way. Please remember for all you non-business people reading this part of the book, client mapping is like dating; if you do your research and target correctly, you can end up with a much better potential partner.

In terms of business, though, I mentioned earlier that while I was in the investment world, there was one year I brought in $1.75 billion of new business, a large proportion of which came from just a few very well-targeted and very large clients.

At the time, I looked after one company called Jupiter Asset Management, which is a fantastic firm with fantastic people. Jupiter had a fund of funds portfolio (which is basically an investment portfolio, like a pension that invests in other company funds. And by fund I mean a portfolio of stocks and shares, or a portfolio of bonds, which is debt or a portfolio of property). They had £12 billion under management— in other words, in the portfolio. The leader of the team was a super guy called John Chatfeild-Roberts, who had actually written a book on investing in mutual funds, so he was one of the brightest minds in the industry. Within that portfolio, they had European equity (company shares) funds exposure of around 10 percent, which meant £1.2 billion in funds comprised of European company shares. And within that 10 percent, they had four different funds almost equally weighted. I knew that they were interested in our European equity fund, so that meant every single time I had a meeting with them, there was a potential new business opportunity of £300 million that could come into our European equity fund. In terms of client mapping, this was a great client to have, because, for the same amount of work as other clients, I could get a much bigger deal into our funds. To put it in perspective, if anyone on my team got a deal of £1 million in a day, it was considered a decent-sized deal, and there would be celebrations. In fact, I already had one deal from them into our Emerging Market Debt fund, which had now grown to £280 million, making them one of our largest clients in our company. I had successfully brokered this deal a few years beforehand and am telling you this so you understand the importance of really researching and knowing your clients, then treating them like friends in order to create trust. Plus, to have success in selling; research the market, so that you find the top targets in terms of clients and then research the individual decision makers within the company, so that you understand the psychology of why they would buy your product. I always say in terms of knowledge; know your client, know your product, and know your industry, and match your client's needs to your USPs, which means unique selling points. Never knock the competition, and if they already have a product with someone else, always compliment their choice because they made that choice for a reason. Sometimes, successful selling can come in the future, and that can mean after a long-term relationship has been developed. Also, client knowledge can lead to awareness in terms of organizational awareness (i.e. what are the different entities within the firm), team awareness (i.e. who are the characters within each team and how do they make decisions), product awareness (in other words what are they interested in, in terms of similar products and why?) and market awareness (what is happening in the current climate and how can your products serve them in this environment). Awareness is key and can help you understand the client's expectations, values and needs.

I talked about the word "leadership" earlier. Well, let's look at the word "relationship" in terms of client relationship or even a personal relationship. The word "relationship" can be broken down into three different parts or words. These include: "Rela" or relay, "Tion" which can mean condi"tion"s or expecta"tion"s and the word "ship." Let's expand out on each of these. Like I described before with the word leadership, a "ship" travels port to port in a direction, and when two people or companies are in a good relationship they are onboard together, traveling in the same direction of where the relationship needs to go and work. I also mentioned that old sailing ships had sails to harness the wind energy. In a client relationship, the more sales you do in terms of positive communication between the two parties, the more likely the relationship will work, as there will be a positive energetic bond between you. But remember, sales is not just about pushing your products and ideas onto people; it is about understanding their needs and matching them with what you have to offer. With a love relationship, it is important to keep the positive communication ongoing with each other, in order to make it a long-term relationship and long-term partnership. On top of this, in order to optimize communication between any two people or two parties, it is very important to understand each other's "tions" i.e. conditions, expectations, needs and values within the relationship. To do this, you need to "rela" or 'relay' through conscious communication; asking the right questions and actively listening to understand what your partner's expectations, needs, and values are. Once obtained, analyze and understand them to see if there is a match with you and you align. We all have our own love languages, and the way we like to be communicated with or to. This is why it is so important to put ourselves in the other person's perspective and speak to them from their love language or their communication style, rather than assuming ours is the same. Relationships are based around positive energy and connection between two people, and that means clear and concise communication and a sense of trust between the two parties. It is also important to read between the lines of what the person is saying, so you truly hear the meaning behind the words, and not just listen to be able to repeat what they said. Communication is about the audio, what you hear, the visual, what you see, and the kinesthetic, what you feel. Conscious communication is so important when engaging with clients, staff, and loved ones. Too often in relationships, people have an opinion, and they push their opinion, make judgements and make assumptions, without seeking to ask the right questions, to first understand the other person's perspective. This has been the cause of love relationships ending, world wars in the past starting, and failure in gaining new business clients. So often, I have seen business people push their products in a sales pitch without even first asking what the client wants or needs. This can be the same in a romantic relationship; where one person just talks at the other person, and then the other does the same back, without actually listening to a word the other person just said. They have their own agendas, and they do not use emotional intelligence to show empathy and understanding in order to seek out what the other person truly needs, wants, and expects. Failure in relationships happens when expectations do not match with reality, and this normally accumulates from a lack of good communication.

In business, it is so important to know everything about the client and how they think, so that you can communicate with them in the way that suits them, rather than what you think suits them. It will save you time and money. What I mean by this, is that there are audio, visual, and kinesthetic people. People who communicate better; through hearing, or through seeing or through getting the feel for something. You also have people with different character types, such as those who are analytical, where they are logical thinkers who can be organized and systematic. Or another character type is a 'driver'; where these people tend to be independent thinkers who can be strong-willed and result-orientated. A third character type are 'expressive' people; who can be opinionated, emotional, and attention-seeking. Finally, there are 'amicable' people who are cooperative, supportive, good listeners, and people-focused. Being able to decipher these personality types can be really helpful in understanding how best to communicate with them. You can develop much quicker rapport with certain people if you hone into the type of person they are and tailor your communication skills and pace of talk, so that they can understand you more easily. It can be called 'mirroring', and it is an excellent way of developing a quick connection with people. I still believe, though, that being your authentic self is the most important thing in the long-term. Imagine you have mastered the art of mirroring lots of different people with different traits, then you go to a conference and four different personality types of people come up to you at the same time to say hello, and they all know each other. Which personality trait do you portray? The other three guys are going to be wondering, Who is this guy? That's why it is still important to remain as you, the true you— let's face it: it's the easiest act to play. The art of mirroring is best used just as an initial introduction where you meet them where they are, their pace, their tone, their communication, and then once you get to know them, you then can slowly bring yourself back to your true style and your true self.

Going back to my Jupiter Asset Management story. In 2011, my fund management company I worked for had a rogue trader in their emerging market debt team, basically a dishonest dealer. It was well-publicized in the press, so I'm not giving anything away, when I tell the story. There was a particular guy on the team doing a transaction with a foreign brokerage at the other end of the deal. He was buying and paying foreign stock at a much higher price than the stock was worth, and the foreign brokerage at the other end was going to bank the difference as profit. It was a scam and illegal. Thankfully, the risk systems in place stopped the deal before it went through. However, the U.K. financial conduct authority did a very thorough investigation after the event, and there was a lot of stress in terms of extra reporting for the team. This excess work and stress for the team took its toll, and by early 2012, the whole team, bar one, decided to leave, to go to another company. Imagine a Formula One racing team losing their star driver and all but one of the team. My CEO at the time said the money in our fund would go and we would lose the business. I felt differently as I had a strong loyal relationship with Jupiter. I set myself up into a knowing state in terms of mindset with the goal of keeping the money. Before any news had gone to press, I immediately phoned Jupiter to tell them the news. This was a good move, as it energetically showed that I cared about them and created trust. I told them that we still had a super fund manager in the driving seat, which was true, and, would they give us the opportunity to re-pitch for the business. They agreed. I also asked would they allow me to bring in my European Fund Manager, to pitch that fund as well, as if they didn't like the new emerging market fund manager, at least they might move the money within our funds, which would limit them in terms of capital gains tax. Before going in, I sat down with our new fund manager and tutored him on all the reasons Jupiter had bought in the first place, their psychology of investing, and any other knowledge that would help him in the meeting. I also trained him in presentation skills, as I was the top presenter in terms of pitching within the business. He was a very capable investor, the only issue was, he was Brazilian, and his English wasn't perfect, which is critical when explaining how you do what you do. The big pitch day arrived, and we went in to the meeting. During the meeting, the Brazilian fund manager was very bland in his communication, and his energy was low because he was nervous and speaking a second language. I could see the three fund managers at the other side of the table were not impressed, and their energy was low, too. It didn't look promising. At this point in the meeting, I started to breath very deeply into my heart with love and positivity and send that energy out to my Brazilian fund manager and the three Jupiter guys. I visualized us winning the deal; I also visualized a connective energy of positivity binding the three guys and my fund manager. Suddenly, out of nowhere, my fund manager seemed to spark up with a new positive energy that he hadn't had before. He started to passionately talk about stocks and how he analyzes them. The three Jupiter guys' energy also changed; their posture became more upright, looking more interested. It was incredible—my energetic intention had worked. We finished the pitch, and then my European Fund Manager came in and pitched afterwards. Again, I held space, sending positive energy to all.

I walked out of the meetings not knowing what their decision was going to be. A week later, I got a phone call saying they liked the new fund manager and they were going to keep the money with us. On top of that, they were really impressed how I had handled the whole situation and had also decided to invest into the European Fund as well. That year, we went from a potential loss of £280 million to a gain in new business of an extra £530 million into the two funds. My CEO and Chairman of my company sent me emails saying they could not believe it and said it was the greatest turnaround the company had ever seen, considering the circumstances. I used a positive mindset to create the goal and outcome I wanted, I took very focused and positive action, I used my knowledge of the client to good effect, and I enthused massive positive energy during the meeting, in order to change the direction of where their decision looked it might be going. The main point of this overall story or example is to showcase the importance of knowing your key clients inside out, and working with them with the utmost respect and integrity.

Also making sure you communicate effectively with them like they are your best friend. Client map to find the key clients and then deliver the best possible service, value and care to keep them. This is the same with any relationship in life. Quite often, once people are in an established relationship, they don't treat the other person in the same way as at the start of the relationship. If you treat a client or a love partner in the same enthusiastic, loving manner that you did when you first won them over, then they will very likely be your partner in business or in life forever.

Another example of how to build successful relationships in business came from J.P. Morgan. I was working for a fund management company and had been regularly pitching our Asian Equity Fund to them. Eventually, the Asian analyst from J.P. Morgan came over from New York to London on a week-long trip to interview around twenty different funds managers. They were looking to decide who they were going to put on their buy list as a fund for J.P. Morgan worldwide. Elizabeth was the analyst, and when she came into our offices, it was the end of the day. She had already seen six fund managers all around London, doing an hour of interviewing with each one, so I could see she was tired. Our fund manager was a lovely person and very capable, but not the best presenter, and her performance was good, but probably not the best in the market. Let's just say she would have been ranked in the top twenty percent, but not number one. Having said that, she was a very stable pair of hands in terms of investing. At the end of the meeting, Elizabeth had to head back to the other side of London, and I escorted her down in the lift from the meeting room and asked her in reception how she was going to get back to her offices. She told me she was going to get a taxi. It was rush hour, and I knew she could end up being stuck in traffic for a long time, and it would be much quicker on the underground. So, I offered to escort her to the underground station, as she didn't know where it was. The walk from our offices was around eight minutes, but during that time, I asked her all about her own self, all about her interests, and all about what she was intending to do while in London, giving her a few tips of fun things to do on the way. I was friendly, kind, and helpful, and I was a gentleman in respect to helping her get a ticket and showing her the way to go.

A week later, I got a call to say we had been successful to get the fund on the buy list. A couple of years later, I was having lunch with Elizabeth, and by this time J.P. Morgan had given us almost $1 billion into that fund. They had become one of our best clients worldwide. I asked her, "Considering there were so many other funds you could have chosen with better results, why did you choose our fund?" She said, "Doug, I was so tired by the end of that day and just wanted to get back to my hotel as quickly as possible, and during my whole trip, you were the only salesperson who left their office to help me. Your genuine kindness made an impression on me, and that was my deciding factor. I knew that you would always endeavor to give us the best possible service and how one person conducts themselves in a company in my viewpoint is an indication of how everyone will act".

What this shows is that in business or in life, if you come from a heart space and genuinely go the extra mile for your clients, your partners, your colleagues, or whoever; they will remember that effort, and you never know, it could lead you to an eight-minute billion-dollar walk.

I always go the extra mile for my clients to add a little extra value for them in any way I can, and I would suggest you always do so as well.

One more important point for success in business is to always remember that everyone in the business is important. When you walk into the reception, always treat the receptionist like he or she is incredibly important. Engage with them, ask them all about themselves, as they probably know everyone in the business, and if you make a good impression with them, you might find that goodwill gets talked about after you leave. Also remember it's not just your network, it's also your network's network that is important. For example, the waiter that serves you in a restaurant might have an off day with you, but could be one of your top client's family. So always treat everyone with respect and care.

I had another client called Scottish Widows Investment Partnership, which got bought out a few times and now is part of the Standard Life group. I was promoting different funds to their team of analysts; and even though I only had three funds that were probably of interest to them, I still met with all of their analysts in all of the areas of the business. I also met with their assistants, their managers, and even met one of the secretaries. You may ask why? The reason was; I wanted to create a positive energy around my company, my products, and myself. I also knew, that even though there were specific decision makers for specific funds, they all still got together as a team when deciding which funds to add onto their buy list. So, the fact that they all knew me and my company, rather than just the one specific analyst, made it a much easier for them to decide as a team; to choose my fund over a competitor. It took me almost three years from when I took over the account to actually getting business from them, but when I did, it was a lump sum of £285 million, which was a massive deal and one of the best wins in the industry that year. It took persistence, a positive mindset, positive energy, a lot of getting to know their entire team, so they all had good knowledge of me and my business to MAKE it happen and seal the deal. Never give up on your goals. Always aim for long-term relationships and see the result in your mind's eye, and keep that vision always in place, and you will have success in business and in life.

As a business owner, I now find social media a very powerful tool as a lead magnet for new coaching and training clients. You can target top clients and business leaders on platforms like LinkedIn, following them, commenting on their posts, and making a connection with them. As an example, I made a strong connection with the president of one of the largest tech firms in the world on LinkedIn. He was promoted, and

I congratulated him, saying that if there was anything I could ever do to add value for him, it would be an absolute pleasure. I added a link to a video of me presenting at the National Workplace Wellbeing Conference in the message, just to showcase me in action and so he could see where I might be able to help. He came back to me in no time whatsoever, and we set up a meeting.

Before the meeting, I thoroughly researched all about him, understanding his interests in work, but also outside of work, too. It is so important to remember that even the most successful people in the world are still human beings with families, friends, and like to have fun. I went into the meeting with the energetic aim of making friends with this guy, not to sell or even come across as if I was selling. Even if he didn't buy from me, I wanted to leave a positive impression where if he was ever asked an opinion of me as a character, his response would be positive. I went into the meeting prepared and with a positive mindset that I was about to make a new friend. When I went in, I said to him that I had read that he was the president of the American Chamber of Commerce in Europe and that I had spoken as keynote speaker at the Dublin, the European, the Galway, and the Tanzanian Chamber of Commerce and that if I could add value with a keynote in the future for him, I would be delighted to support. I also mentioned that I had read he was a member for the Special Olympics committee in Ireland. I was an ambassador for a charity that supported children with disabilities and offered collaboration in any way to support him and what he did. I also mentioned I knew he had two children who were a similar age to mine, that he was a rugby fan like myself, and we had common friends in business. It all was to establish a positive connection with common interests and goals in life as well as business. It was genuine interest and a genuine energetic intention of wanting to make friends, and to connect on a heart level. He could feel that energy, and that automatically created trust and rapport. He also could see I had done my research, showing a genuine interest in him. This is key with any relationship, whether in business or in life, because if you show genuine heart felt interest in others they will show interest in you too. He then invited me into his office and once the common interests and connection had been established, I then asked him permission to tell him a little about my consulting business. This is a very important factor in any business relationship; because by asking permission to sell before actually selling, it will engage any listener much more. It shows respect for his time and his attention and subconsciously, he will listen with more focus. It is also good manners, rather than just going into a pitch straightaway.

Once, I began; never once did I say how good my company was, my consultants were, or how good I was. I used LinkedIn testimonies written by CEOs and senior executives from similar companies, to showcase the results that I had before and proving the value of my work. This is something I highly suggest all businesspeople do. Also, in relationship dating, previous dates have checked them out as well. Once I had showcased my and my team's skills using testimonies, he told me he would like to bring me into the business for coaching, consulting, and corporate training, and he gave me names of people to contact. I shook his hand with gratitude, walked out of the office, got into my car, and drove five minutes away to the nearest service station and pulled in. I immediately wrote him an email thanking him for his time and made three short bullet points of where I could add value to him and his business. This incredible gentleman came back to me within ten minutes, linking in all the relevant people in human resources, and the rest is history. I have been coaching and consulting there ever since, for almost three years now. The quick email follow-up was key, as I was still fresh in his memory, and my energy was still in his field. Again, this is an example of positive mindset with the intention of making a new friend, not selling. People can feel it when you are just trying to sell to them. He knew; I was genuine about wanting to add value and create friendship;

he could feel that vibe. I took focused action to learn all about him, and then showcased this knowledge to show genuine interest in him. Finally, I went in with a high degree of positive energy to MAKE it happen. All of this being genuine love and care for another human being, and pure positive intention of creating a long-term relationship. This works in business and in life.

In this case targeting the President of a global technology firm is a prime example of client mapping, creating relationships, and building connections in a positive way.

It led to my first executive coaching client at the company; who was a super guy who managed over 300 people. The original assignment was to help him with his interpersonal relations and his communication skills within the company. That rapidly expanded out to conscious leadership, teamworking skills, presentation skills, energy management, stress management, and performance management. Sometimes, people in life come with one issue, but when you peel back the layers by asking the right questions to understand and develop trust; other underlying issues can pop up. It is so important to treat clients, colleagues, and team members with respect and appreciation and really try to understand everything from their perspectives as well as your own, in order to add as much value as possible. It was supposed to only be a one-year contract, but he rolled it over for a second year, as I must have added some value, and we are still friends today.

My next main coaching client at the same company was a C-level executive in his sixties, another super guy who managed over 1,200 people at one stage. This was a guy up the hierarchy and I was delighted to get him as client, as it meant my reputation of producing positive results was being communicated across the company. Proof of concept in terms of the results is key in any business. Treat every client as if they are your most important client and always have their back. Be there for them when they need you, and have the intention of making them long-term friends. You might wonder why a C-level executive would want a coach. I have said it before and I will say it again; the best sports people in the world have coaches, not because the coach is a better player; they are just good at masterminding people up to a higher level of performance. Plus, sometimes we need a third-party perspective to see the things that we sometimes don't see in ourselves. It is so important to look at all areas of a person's life to enable them to be in the best energetic state physically, mentally, emotionally, and even spiritually, so that they perform to the highest level.

Sometimes, you may find people you manage, lead or coach will give you pushback on your style of coaching or leadership and as long as you create trust, rapport, always aim to add value and come from a heart space they usually will come around.

I had one client years ago who was a C-level investment guy at one of the biggest investment banks in the world. He was one of the most influential investment managers in the industry and extremely clever. I had specifically targeted him as a key client, and it took many phone calls and much persistence to get his time for a one-hour meeting. Eventually, when we met, he went into a lot of technical jargon to try to sound intelligent and baffle me. In that hour conversation, I would say I spoke for five minutes of the time, asking interested questions, and checking back on what he said to understand. The rest of the time he spoke.

After the meeting, he rang my boss, as they used to work together, and told him that I was one of the most intelligent and talented salespeople he had ever met. All I did was let him speak, then I showed genuine interest in what he was saying and made him feel good through asking some specific questions. We went on to become good friends, and he gave me a lot of business. Always remember: God gave you two ears and one mouth, and to use them in that proportion when conversing with others, especially in business. You don't necessarily have to understand what a person is saying in totality, as long as you listen intently and get the general meaning, so that they will feel you care. Also remember that people love to talk about themselves, so ask questions, let them talk, and show genuine interest.

Good questions I find to ask with a new client or radio guest include:

"I love meeting successful or interesting people like yourself. How did you become the success that you are today?"

"Successful people like yourself always seem to have a wealth of experience and learnings that we can learn from. What do you think were your biggest learnings, that you had, along the way?"

"Now that you have become this incredible success and you know what you know, what advice would you give your younger eighteen-year-old self?"

"You are now a model to so many in your industry. I'd love to know who have been your biggest models or influencers along the way?"

"As a person who is obviously very well-read, what books would you recommend that helped you on your path of success and why?"

"You have amazing energy; how do you get and keep yourself in this high vibe state?"

And then a more personal question which can create good rapport is; "I am always fascinated to ask what successful people like you do for fun or to relax when you are not working?"

What you will note is that with each of these questions, I first compliment the person before asking the question. It is to recognize the value I put on their answer before asking the question. It is a very good way to get people to want to help you and want to fully answer.

If you meet someone new, try focusing on asking these questions, and then, when they feed back their answers, listen intently, and see if there are further sub-questions you can ask to get them to open up and talk about themselves. It is a great way of showing interest, creating rapport, and getting to know the other person. Most people get asked are they married or do they have kids, which are nice questions if you are married and do have kids, but not so appropriate if you don't. Instead, using the above questions can be a great way to truly get an understanding of other person's true self and create a more meaningful interaction and potential friendship. The power of questioning and listening skills helps in all aspects of communication; and conscious communication is one of the keys to charging yourself up for success. Success in relationships, business, and life all comes from the power of your communication skills and understanding the other person's perspective to get more done in less times with less stress. This is something I teach people every single day.

In terms of saving time, let's go back to client mapping. Map out who your key clients are and then call them with the intention of meeting face to face. Once you meet them, you can connect with them on the audio (speech and hearing), visual (seeing) and kinesthetic (touch through a handshake, a hug, or a pat on the arm). In the first meeting, ask questions to understand them, learn about their needs, goals, dreams, and wishes, and then, see if you can collaborate to help them get those needs. Remember, relationships are built on an exchange of energy. Seek to give first to add value, then once trust and rapport has been established, then you will find the other person will give back to you as well.

When I was in the investment world, every year, I was given a target in terms of business I had to bring in. I had researched, mapped out, and developed a good knowledge of my client base, their potential, what kind of products they were interested in, and when they were looking for new funds like ours to buy. The clients were large financial institutions and the aim was to get funds on their buy lists and then convince the portfolio managers to buy them. I needed knowledge of the right people to speak to, which I often found out by making friends with competitor sales managers, collaborating and sharing ideas. Always remember that collaboration is better than competition. I said it before, and I will say it again: where there is competition, there is a sense of lack, as if you are gunning or going for the same thing; whereas, with collaboration, you can work together to create new things from nothing. Find out which other product or service providers work with your clients and see if you can work together to add even more value to these clients.

As a radio presenter, I often speak to other presenters or podcasters and find out who were their best guests that they have interviewed, and I share mine too. It adds value to the other presenter and also adds value to the guest, as they get to advertise their services on another platform. You can do the same whatever business you are in. Think abundance, think added value to the client and let go of fear. Yes, learn from the competition, but do not fear them.

Activity planning:

Once you have a good pipeline of clients through client mapping, the next task, which is so important to help you achieve your business goals, is activity planning.

Activity planning in business is incredibly important for time management. We all, only get a certain number of hours in the day, so how you use these hours is paramount. Some people are busy getting nothing done and some people even spend hours in the office just to trying to look good. They arrive either at the same time as the boss and leave either just after the boss leaves or at the same time, so that they can chat to them on the way out. This is fine if the production and output is good, but really any business owner doesn't really care about who's done the most hours; they want to know who is the most productive and who creates the most positive results. I always aim to get as much done as possible in the shortest space of time and make sure the activities I do lead directly towards my goals or the company's goals.

In terms of a daily habits in this activity planning, I would highly advise that you do your administration in the morning when you're fresh, in other words getting the boring stuff out of the way. Then, if you're in sales, get your meetings done in and around lunchtime. If you can, put your most important meeting for the day at lunchtime, itself, because everybody has to eat, and the customer will give you a bit more time and will probably be more relaxed during the meeting. Quite often these days, people utilize the lunchtime to play sport, go to the gym, and exercise. You can always join them. I used to play squash and go to the gym with clients, which was a great way to bond with them.

Then, put two geographically close clients as meetings on either side of your lunch, so that you optimize your time out of the office. Perhaps, you might have an 11 a.m., a 12:30 p.m., and a 2:30 p.m. meeting. This is good planning and good use of time and by having those three meetings during the mid-part of your day, you will get you into the flow of talking about the markets, industry, current affairs, and products. Then, when you get back to the office, it might be a fantastic time to make sales calls because you can use this knowledge, and add value to the clients on the phone. You will also have a sense of self confidence through the market and industry knowledge you acquired. I often would say on the phone to a client, "I just met with one of the top companies like your own at lunchtime, and we were talking about XYZ…". This is a great way to catch the attention of the person on the phone, as they always want to know what their competitors are up to. You don't have to give names or details, just general industry insight to gain interest. In terms of sales calls on the phone, I always found clients are busy doing their own administration in the morning and they tended to be much more relaxed in the afternoon, which I also think is because they are going home soon, so they are happier. When making a call, I rarely would try to sell on the phone, as when you call someone, you are disturbing them from the work they are doing in that moment. My aim was always to value their time and use the call to arrange a face-to-face meeting with them over the next few weeks, where I would then develop the client relationship with them in the way I discussed before. Once this call was made, I would then follow up with an email with a thanks for their time, confirmation of the meeting, and a short outline of how I will add value when we meet. Keep the information in the email concise, preferably with a few bullet point highlights with the most important information. That way, if they just read the bullet points, your impact and time is worthwhile. Let's face it: most buyers in any industry will be bombarded with emails on a daily basis. It's much better to send an email as a follow-up, because they know you, rather than a cold email out of the blue. Also, when someone sees a title of the email something to the extent of "following on from our call," they tend to look at that ahead of a 'product titled' email. Activity mapping helps you make sure that you are spending the right time with the right people and doing all the tasks that can produce the highest potential in terms of results. Time is our most important asset, so value it and plot out what are the tasks you can spend time on that move you the most quickly towards your goals.

In business PR is also incredibly important for you and your company; whether a multi-national or even a small company. Advertising can be expensive, so why not write thought pieces, market observations, and industry views that relate to your products in some way or form that will add value to others. Then, send them to trade newspapers and national newspapers. A lot of these papers are crying out for content, and your article will be free advertising for you and your business. I did this with one of my financial services companies that I worked for, and we won an award for Global Brand of the Year because we got so much press in the trade and national newspapers. You can also put in articles on every new joiner you have and write something nice about them mentioning all the companies they worked for in the past. That way the online keyword searches for all of those companies might bring up your article as well, giving you more exposure. Newspaper articles about a new joiner also make the new joiner feel important and good about joining your company. It will also make them feel even more valued and in turn, help create a dedicated new employee who feels accountable to the public as well as your company.

These ideas in terms of activity planning are applicable to most types of businesses, that are looking to grow. What about, if you are only just starting out, and want to creating a new business. Or what activity planning can you do to help you start a side hustle or a passive income stream? Here's one answer…

The entrepreneur business model that you can use to create passive income as a full-time or side-business:

We all have experiences in life or business that we can use to add value to people in some way or form. I, for example, had a near-death experience and various stress-related issues, so that gave me a chance to learn how to create success without stress and learn to heal myself and others through body, mind and soul techniques. I also played with, and coached some of the top hockey players in the world and had a successful track record in sales and leadership. On top of these, I have presented on stages all over the world and interviewed some of the most inspiring people on my radio show. So, these experiences have helped me to learn the highest quality of communication and presentation skills. I now use these skills to help other people in their jobs, businesses, relationships and in media as well. I also have an online course to help people in a similar way to this book.

I am sure you, yourself, have something to share, something that you know that maybe others don't. Or through your own experience and differing perspective you can add value to people in some way or form. It could be to do with relationships, parenting, business, sport, art, or music. For example, I helped one lady who designed jewelry for people to put a video together to show people how she made the jewelry, so that people could do it themselves. She made money from selling her jewelry and money from how she made it. Really think outside of the box, and don't fear that you are giving away any secrets. That is just ego. Share your knowledge with the intention of helping and supporting others. You may just become a recognized expert in your field.

Here's how you can share your knowledge online to add value, touch hearts and make a bit of money on the way:

STEP 1:

Take your knowledge that you know would add value to people and create a PowerPoint presentation course on it, so that people can learn from your experiences, model your success, and do the same thing for themselves. This could even be tips on alternative healing methods you may have used to cure an ailment or tips on how you grew a million-dollar business. Make the course last between three to four hours with precise and easy-to-follow content. It is always good to use practical examples from your own experiences that the audience can relate to. Once you are ready to deliver the course, hire a videographer for the day and go to a hotel meeting room or nice setting and deliver it, videoing yourself in the process. You can even take the transcript of what you say and put it into a book for an extra source of income. You can use the Otter app to do an initial transcript and then send it to an editor to quickly and efficiently produce a booklet or even a book. Once the course has been edited by yourself or the videographer, put the course onto a platform, so that it can be bought by the public. The subject matter of the course is always better if it is slightly unique, or in a niche. There are so many personal development and learning courses out there, so find your unique selling point and target audience. You can use platforms like Kajabi, Udemy, or Teachable, just to name a few, to host your course. Charge something reasonably affordable, then advertise using Facebook and Google advertisements. The price of the course depends on the market, the quality and how much you value yourself.

STEP 2

Start up a podcast or radio show, so that you can interview inspiring people or experts in their field, learn from them, and make friends with them. This might lead to great opportunities in terms of speaking engagements and other collaborations. When you are seeking to get these guests on your show, use LinkedIn as a way of messaging them. I find that a lot of celebrities have social media assistants for most platforms, but less so for LinkedIn, as there are corporate business opportunities there, and these corporations like to deal with the real people.

STEP 3

Set up a Facebook or LinkedIn group that is subscription-based where you get people in and then charge them for your advice. You could put a subscription of, say, $5 a month, the price of a coffee, then advertise the group as mentioned above. Then, add value in the group through video coverage of your podcast guests, webinars every week of yourself presenting, and presentations answering maybe three questions a week from different people within the group through a live video. The total time investment each week may be as little as two hours.

STEP 4

Set up an online mastermind or networking group to do with your specialty area and charge a yearly subscription for the mastermind, which will be much higher than the above support group. You can then bring in your podcast guests as speakers to add value, and you can do a question-and-answer session afterwards. This would add value to the speaker, as well as your mastermind group, as you are providing an audience for them which is a really good way of collaborating. Plus, audiences love to interact with successful people, so it is WIN-WIN all around. Make sure you record and transcribe the mastermind, and then, you can use the content for other purposes.

## STEP 5

Do live seminars, webinars, or summits online where you can charge people for your knowledge based around what you have already put together in all of the above. Remember there is so much information out there, so workshop exercises to give people experiences, games, and practices during their time with you, will make them enjoy the event so much more.

## STEP 6

Seek out conference organizers, summit organizers, and even senior company executives who bring in paid speakers to add value to their events.

## STEP 7

Offer high level one-on-one coaching, consulting, or healing. Remember, this can be time-consuming, as you are giving up your time for one person when you could be using your skillset to help many more people in that same hour. Having said that, there is nothing more satisfying than working closely with people who need help and seeing their lives change in a positive way. Life isn't about money; it is about adding value and touching lives. Based on this, I would always try and keep one-on-one clients as well, especially if you have a skillset like healing; it is your gift given to you, so use it with love.

With the book, I would also encourage you to have an audiobook, as it gives another channel of passive income. You can read it yourself, or you can get someone to read it for you, at a reasonable price.

This is a business model that has opportunities for passive income at multiple levels and works whether you are an energy healer or a financial advisor. Just remember, it may cost you to get some of the above steps done, but, if it all works out and adds value, it will only take one professional speaking gig paying you five figures to get all your money back in one go.

# MASTERING THE ART OF CREATING GOALS THROUGH ENERGETIC INTENTION

If you have been following the actions in the last few chapters, you will hopefully have a business plan or life plan in place and some grounded ideas on how to achieve it. The question is; how can we use what we learnt in the earlier chapters in respect to energy and intention to create your goals more efficiently? The below goalsetting tips show steps that many of my radio guests and my own self have used to create the life we wanted, and they might just help you too…

1. **Once you know what your goal is and you have it very clearly defined in your mind, visualize the goal, and regularly keep the thought of the goal in your mind.** The goal is always energetically easier if it is aligned to your true sense of purpose in life, which we talked about earlier. Goals that are not aligned to your true purpose can sometimes become a distraction from what you are meant to do on this planet. You can achieve them, of course, but goals that are aligned to your true sense of purpose seem to just happen with so much more ease, and the satisfaction of achieving them will be much stronger. This is why you get a lot of people setting goals to do with money and fame, which once they have achieved them, they

do not feel fulfilled within. So many people say "I'll be happy when I get this" or "I will be happy when I achieve that", then they get it or achieve that and they still aren't happy. Success without fulfillment is not really success. So, once you know, your true purpose or have created a sense of purpose based around adding value to others, then the more you think about the goal, the more ideas will come into your head to help you make it happen. Also, by being in the energy frequency of the goal, in terms of thinking about it, you will naturally attract like vibrational experiences and people into your life. That's why they say; if one of your goals is to attract a perfect love partner, then write down all the character traits of the love partner that you want, and then go out and act like those traits yourself. For example, if you wanted a partner with a fit body, then maybe you should go down to the gym and work on one yourself. Also, you never know, you may just meet your soul mate in that gym. Alternatively, if in business, and you want to attract a particular client; find out through research, what the client likes to go to in terms of trade fairs or conferences and then turn up at them and introduce yourself. People like people who are like them, so try and get to know as much as you can about the person you want to attract into your life, whether in business or in love.

 Visualization can be used to put yourself into the energy of what you want for your future self and it can be very powerful. I had an experience recently where I was presenting as the main keynote speaker for the Institute of Directors, India at their Global convention in London for Sustainability and climate change. There were some of the most successful Indian businessmen in the world there; including the Chairman of Oil and Gas India and the CEO of Cobra Beer. While I was there I was surrounded by lovely Indian people talking about sustainability and climate change. I also was thinking about my daughter as I hadn't seen her in a little while and was dreaming of her reaching out to me.

The next day, after the event, I left my hotel and went to Heathrow airport as I normally travel with the airline I was with, from there. When I got there, I realized I had made mistake and I should have been at Gatwick airport instead. I had no idea how I had made that mistake as I had never done it before. I changed my ticket and got onto the plane in Heathrow. I sat down in the window seat of the airplane and next to me was a father with his one-year-old daughter on his lap and she kept reaching out to me on the flight. I got chatting to the Dad and found out he was one of the leading sustainability consultants in Europe and sitting next to him on the other side was his wife, who was Indian. So, I was in the energy of lovely Indian people, thinking about my daughter reaching out and talking about sustainability and hey presto; I attracted that energy into my future. Get into the energy and the feeling of what you want and watch the magic, that can happen.

In my experience of using visualization, I mentioned earlier on, that, when I was younger, I was the southeast of England 100 meter running champion. I was thirteen years of age, and despite being one of the smaller runners, I was the fastest. I was so determined to win that I would visualize myself winning before the race even started. I would also say out loud that I was going to win over and over again, before a race, and sure enough, I won time and time again. In fact, it was only when the other boys started to grow, and my father said to me that he couldn't believe I was still winning with the size of some of those other guys, that things changed.

The next time I went up to the starting lineup, I looked across and saw the size of the guy next to me. That day I came second. Why? Because my mind went into a state of fear and doubt. It is so important to focus purely on the end goal, the finishing line and not on the distractive thoughts that get in the way. Staying in that knowing mindset, knowing you are going to win is crucial.

In terms of a knowing mindset, Roger Bannister was one of the top U.K. athletes who used to run the mile back in the 1950s. And before 1954, no one had ever achieved the four-minute mile. In 1954, Roger broke the four-minute mile mark. Once he had broken it for the first time, something remarkable happened—just 46 days later, John Landy broke it again and was a second faster. Within a few years, four people would break the four-minute mile in a single race. How? Because now they had a knowing mindset, they knew they could achieve it, as it already had been done. I have said before, and I will say it again to repeat and seed your subconscious; often what stops us in life is fear. If you can get yourself out of your head and into your heart you will come from a place of love rather than fear.

2. **Write your goals down in "I am grateful" statements, as if you have already achieved them and add in; how it adds value to others as well as yourself.** The reason people use 'I am' statements comes from the Bible from when Moses sees God and asks, "What is your name, Lord?" and God says, "I am that I am." So, the belief is that whatever you say after 'I am', you can create it energetically through the power of your voice. It is also stated in the Bible that you should always pray for things in gratitude. Plus, by writing it down, you are seeding it into the subconscious mind, especially if you write your goals down often and say them out loud as affirmations again and again. By saying them out loud, you are resonating the vibrational energy out into the atmosphere with the intention of creation, but also when you say it, you will also hear it, and it goes back into your mind as an affirmation and even an incantation. I once heard it said, that 'your word is your wand' so use it wisely.

The final part of the puzzle is to use your full name in the sentence alongside the I am grateful statement. The reason behind this is spiritual, and you can take it or leave it. For myself, having had a near-death experience, I believe we have lifetime after lifetime coming back to learn and grow as a soul. And as mentioned earlier in the book, my viewpoint is that we reincarnate over and over again, to live through different perspectives in life: man, woman, king, queen, prince, pauper, invalid, and Olympian. Let's face it: if we are spiritual beings wanting to experience a life in physical form, in this space suit we call our body, wouldn't we want to try on all the costumes and experience all the angles? Or alternatively, we may also come here to correct karma in terms of being on the other end of the interaction, experiencing both the pain and the pleasure of life. So, it is important in my opinion to ask very precisely for what you wish for as 'you', meaning; using your name, in this life time, in the 'I am' statement. You might ask, what do I mean by that? Well, if you were to use the affirmation, "I am grateful to the Universe that I am a multimillionaire and I own a six-bedroom house with an indoor swimming pool," you might create that in your next life, rather than this one, because, just maybe, the soul doesn't differentiate between this human lifetime and the next. Perhaps, it sees this lifetime as just one chapter in many lifetimes, of your overall soul life. Therefore, in my viewpoint, it is better to make the I am statement, saying; "I am grateful to the Universe that I, Douglas Donald Gordon, am a multimillionaire, and own a six-bedroom house with an indoor swimming pool." Remember, God said his name is "I am that I am," and God is an infinite being, as is your soul. So, in my opinion, this human life of yours is just one in many chapters of your overall life. This is, however, just an opinion based on my near-death experience, and you might not believe in multiple lifetimes; and that is okay. Some people might say that if you have pure intention, in your affirmation, then you will create it anyway, with names or not. You might be correct, but in creating your dream life, why not cover all angles and be specific using your name in your voiced request.

I like to write down "I am grateful" statements for what I have every day, and I also write down "I am grateful" statements as if I already have what I want to manifest as well. For example, when writing this book, I would write down;

"I, Doug Gordon, am grateful that I am an international bestselling author, selling millions of copies of my book worldwide, in order to touch millions of hearts and help people to connect with their best selves, in order to live their best lives. Plus, I am grateful for being paid millions of euros for doing so within the next five years, so that I can use that money to build a healing or retreat center to help even more people."

Now, you may say that this is a bit longwinded, but what happens is if people put an "I am grateful" statement for what they want, such as, "I am grateful that I am a bestselling author." This can be bit too vague, and then there is the possibility that they become a bestselling author for only one day on Amazon because all their friends and family buy their book and nothing else. In other words; they are not specific enough. What I did in my statement is to be very specific, making the statement about adding value to others, so that it is not just a selfish statement to just benefit me; it will help others. That way, by helping and serving others, it gives you a sense of purpose and meaning, which in turn energizes you, even more. On top of this, make your statements time-specific; to set the goal in your own mind to keep yourself accountable and to help you to take focused action towards it.

In terms of being very specific; a few years ago, I had a grateful affirmation of, "I am grateful that I am on TV." I was actually still working in the investment world at the time, and after a few weeks of saying this statement daily, I suddenly found myself getting calls from all around the world asking to do video conferences with me in terms of sales and investment. So, hey, presto… next minute, I'm looking at myself on the screen, on TV. Not what I quite wanted, but the Universe gave me what I asked for. This is why it is so important to be very specific for what you ask for; and if it aligns positively for you and others, watch the magic that can happen. Remember to focus on what you want in terms of the structure of your sentences you use, rather than what you don't want. On a side note, maybe everyone wanted to be on TV in 2019, and maybe that collective consciousness might, and I say might, just have contributed to the COVID-19 pandemic happening because everyone suddenly found themselves working from home on Zoom meetings and in turn, on TV. I am kind of joking, but worth thinking about to get us all being very conscious and very specific about our goals and affirmations.

When I first wanted to get on radio, my intention to do so was so that I could share my near-death experience and help people in some way or form. At the time, I had an "I am grateful statement" that I wrote consistently… "I am grateful that I'm on the radio," and I'd say this over and over again. Then, within one month, I went to present at a presentation skills training conference with around 300 people there. It was interesting, as the guy who introduced me said, "With branding, Doug Gordon can be a global superstar" in terms of public speaking. At the end of that conference, I met a guy in the elevator who had a radio show called "Breakthrough Brands," and within a few weeks, I was on his radio show talking about my near-death experience. Soon after, I was on another radio show, then another one, and within a few months, I had been on seven different radio shows. At this point, someone said to me I had a voice for radio and that I should get my own show. So, I changed my goal and my "I am grateful statement" to say, "*I am grateful that I have my own radio show*." Then, within one month of consistently saying this, I had my own radio show. It was also interesting at the time, as I had another "I am grateful" statement of "I am grateful that I am an inspirational speaker, speaking to millions of people all around the world, adding value to them." Binding these two affirmations together, it is interesting that when I was given the radio show with the radio station, the CEO at the time asked me what I wanted to call the show. I thought about it and said, "The Mindful Millionaire" because I had worked in the stock market and was now into mindfulness. He told me that it was a bit American and not really appropriate for the Irish market, so we sat down came up with, "Inspirational People, Inspirational Stories" and hence, I became an inspirational speaker, as well as getting my radio show! Two "I am grateful" affirmations combined and brought into reality. I have to say I am delighted we chose that name because when I ask anyone to come on my show, they always are delighted – who wouldn't be when you are calling them inspirational?

Another lesson learned from this was "The Mindful Millionaire" was about me; "Inspirational People, Inspirational Stories" is about the guest. Always think in terms of the other person and what's in it for them, rather than yourself, if you want to create a positive outcome. Every week, I research and design the show around adding value to the guest, telling their story to inspire others, then promoting their services and getting their message out to the world. The energetic intention behind me doing the show is to add value to the guest, add value to the listener, and make a new friend with the guest who comes on the show. People can feel that energy, and that is why I get amazing guests on from all over the world. These include incredible people like Dr. John Demartini, Lisa Nichols, and Stephen M.R. Covey—all New York Times bestselling authors. Then there was Tasia Valenza, the Hollywood actress who was in Star Wars and Star Trek, another great guest. Also closer to home, I have had Eamonn Quinn from Ireland, who is one of the Irish TV stars from Dragons' Den, Keith Barry, the famous magician and hypnotist, Pat Falvey, who was the first man in the world to peak the seven summits first, plus reach the north and south poles. Also, Jack Daly, who is one of the top speakers in the area of sales in the world. Jack came to Ireland a month after his wife had died and delivered one of the best speeches I have heard on sales in front of 7,000 people at the Pendulum summit, despite being in mourning. What an incredible guy. These people have become friends and have kindly supported me in many different ways, which I am so grateful for; including giving endorsements for this book.

I have one funny side story about Jack Daly, which I love telling… He came over to Ireland to do a Hyper Sales Growth Conference all about sales and leadership. There were around 300 people there, and it was a one-day event, and he asked for two guest speakers to come in and speak at the event alongside him. One was myself and the other was Gerry Duffy, who ran 32 marathons in 32 consecutive days and also did 10 Ironman events in 10 days, which is pretty impressive for a guy who used to smoke and drink like a trooper. Gerry is one of the top speakers in Ireland and did a talk on goal-setting for businesses. I was doing a talk on how to make sales in your business, based around how I grew an asset management business from $50 million per annum sales to $1.75 billion per annum sales in six years. As a recent ex-corporate guy, I turned up with my computer and a PowerPoint presentation on the day at 7 a.m. Jack took one look at me and said, "Doug, I love you, but, we don't do PowerPoint in my seminars." So, I whizzed out to the reception of the hotel and got a flip chart, that I could use on a stand and proceeded to convert my slides from my PowerPoint onto the flip chart. I returned with a smile on my face, only to be greeted by Jack again, with another question, "Is that just your PowerPoint slides on the flip chart? Do you know it or not? If so, do it with no flip chart and no slides, and prove you are as good as I know you are!" Before throwing away my flip chart, Jack had a good look through all the slides and pages. The guests arrived, and the event began. Jack then proceeded to cover pretty much every topic I had on my flip chart. I was sitting there suddenly very nervous, as I was going to have to come up with a new presentation on the spot. The urge to go to the toilet suddenly heightened dramatically, and the tension in my bottom went sky high. I was not impressed. I decided, I was just going to have to use practical, real-life examples of client interactions; to emphasize the points that Jack was now making and I was going to make. Thankfully, I delivered, it flowed, and I got a standing ovation. Jack came up to me afterwards, put a hand on my shoulder, winked, and smiled at me saying, "Well done. You were fantastic, and I knew you had it in you." Funny afterwards, I guess but I almost shit myself at the time. Quite often, you can be at an event as a speaker, and sometimes the speakers before you can use the same stories as you might be using yourself, so a quick change can be very beneficial, and Jack helped me to learn this the hard way. It also has helped me to think on my feet and present from my heart, rather than my head.

In fact, if you are ever nervous when you are about to speak in public or going into a big meeting, there is a great exercise you can do to get you out of your head-self, your EGO self, and into your heart self, your higher self. What I would do, and you can copy this, is I would put my hand on my heart and say, "I am Doug Gordon. I am my heart. Please let me connect with the hearts of the audience, in order to bless, rather than impress, and add as much value as possible." Then, just visualize love and kindness in your heart and see that energy going out from your heart to all the hearts of the audience. This is a really powerful thing to do because fear comes from ego and normally comes from your head and worried thoughts. Whereas, if you get into a place of love, a place of heart, you cannot have any fear. In turn, you will be less worried about making mistakes, because you are purely aiming to bless, rather than impress.

3. **If possible, voice your goals out loud with someone else who is aligned in wanting the best for you.** Or, like me, is very connected to energy and holds the space for you and affirms, for you, in unison.

    Where focus goes, energy flows. Or, as it says in the Bible... where there are two or more in faith, God will be there. It has been proven in energy healing and in group meditation that the collective consciousness and collective focus on creating something can be energetically very powerful. It is the reason; that when I got a sniff of a deal in the investment world, I would immediately talk about it with my boss, the fund managers, the support staff, anyone who would listen. I did this, to create more energy around the idea, and bring it to life through collective thinking. Your word is your wand, as they say, so the more people incanting the same goal the better. I also believe that by saying something over and over again it seeds the subconscious and creates neuroplasticity within the brain, thus creating a new pattern of thinking, speaking and acting. It also puts you in the energy of what you want to create by talking about it.

    Recently on a holiday, my partner and I were in a car listening to a guy on the radio talk about how doctors are experts in their field, but the field of medicine is ever-evolving. This means doctors don't have time to keep up with the changing treatments because they are so busy helping people. I commented to my partner, "99% of doctors are good people, and they are just doing their best in what they know; to help people, and we shouldn't knock them. They are caring, kind, and hardworking people." Twenty minutes later, we arrived at a mountain for a walk in the middle of nowhere. On our walk, we met a couple and chatted with them along the way. They were French. They were both retired doctors, and they were lovely. They were going to catch a bus back down the mountain to their hotel, which was on our way, so I offered them a lift, and they accepted. We arrived at their hotel, they bought us drinks and lunch, and we had an absolutely lovely conversation with two of the nicest people you could meet. So, as I have said before, I have a true knowing that the words we use and speak can create and it did in this situation. I mentioned doctors are nice people and within a few hours, I am sitting there in front of exactly what I voiced, having lunch with two of them. Always be consciously voicing your goals, and phrase them in a way that creates what you want, rather than what you don't want. Like the example I used earlier where my client asked me to voice and manifest that, "It wouldn't rain on her wedding day," I said no, and instead, I voiced; "that I am grateful there is blue sky and sunshine on her wedding day." This way, I am voicing what she truly wants, rather than what she doesn't want. The words "rain" and "wedding day" in the same sentence would not be a wise combination, in my opinion, even if the sentiment was good and the meaning the same. "Voice what you want, not what you don't want." I believe the subconscious mind doesn't understand "I hope nots," double negatives, and the like. It just hears the words you say and energetically interlinks them to create.

4. **Be grateful for all you have.** I mentioned earlier; when you give a child a present and the child isn't grateful— you don't feel like giving the child anything else. So why would God, the Universe, or even your own subconscious make you feel worthy enough to receive

anything else if you are not truly grateful for what you have already created in your life or that has been given to you in the past? When you are in a state of gratitude for what you have, then this produces more positive energy flow and it increases your positive emotions, i.e. energy in motion, which are key to the creation of future dreams, wishes, and goals. Getting into the vibrational energy of receiving and feeling worthy will bring more abundance towards you. A state of gratitude increases your positive vibe and as we know your vibe attracts your tribe, so you will attract more positive people into your life and more positive happenings too.

5. **Stay aligned and connected to your heart in terms of positivity and positive energy**. If you just say an "I am grateful" statement, or wish with no heart, no emotion, or no meaning, then why would the Universe take you seriously? Whereas, if you do a meditation to connect to your heart self, and then put your hand on your heart and feel the energy flow within your heart with a feeling of love and emotion, you will create powerful 'energy in motion'. Once you have this feeling in place, then say your, "I am grateful" statements with true meaning and passion. That way, you will have a lot more power behind them, and the universal energy will feel that frequency, and that energy vibration will illuminate out, and in turn bring into your field whatever you desire. Like I said earlier, get out of your headspace and into your heart space and come from that place of LOVE with Lots Of Vibrant Energy.

Remember, your vibe attracts your tribe, so always try and keep positive. Because of your past, you will always get the odd family member or friend who doesn't believe you can do it, tries to put you down or tries to hold you back. Don't let negativity and negative people deter you from your positive vibration and attraction of your goals. Don't complain, gossip, or waste any energy on anything that doesn't align with your goals. Always take these people as just tests to see if you are still on track in the game of life. Maybe the Universe is sending you these difficult people to test your faith, your resolve, and your emotional intelligence, to see if you can still play the game of life and win - despite the obstacles that sometimes get in the way. When you start to evolve and grow in life, there may well be family members or friends who will do anything to hold you back, just because they are so afraid of you finding your wings, leaving the nest, and soaring into the sky, leaving them behind. The only thing you can do is to assure them that you will always love them, always be there for them, and will always have a seat on the plane for them. Having said that; you need to ask them to support you in a positive way on your journey, regardless of their views, opinions or the outcome.

Speaking of your "vibe attracts your tribe"—I was on a virtual stage recently doing a mastermind on mental wellness. The room had a lovely feel to it, and there was lots of positivity and kindness being shared to help people with their questions. Suddenly, the moderator made a judgmental comment about another guy giving practical mental wellness advice to help someone. I have to say it was kind of strange, as the advice came from a place of love and from his heart. I understand from her perspective she felt that sometimes people just want to vent, tell their story, and they don't necessarily want advice, but at the same time, the advice was sound, helpful, and kind. Within five minutes of her judgement, there were suddenly new people joining the stage to mastermind with us. The energy completely changed and there were multiple judgements about other people made out of the blue. An uncomfortable feeling was felt across the stage. The energy had completely changed. We all judge situations, people, types of cars, houses, and everything in life sometimes. What I would say is to ask yourself when judging another person is, "Is this judgement coming from my heart, a place of love, or is it coming from a place of ego? And will it uplift the other person and truly help the other person by me relaying my judgement, or is it just going to put them down and satisfy my own ego by telling them so?" In this circumstance, based on where the direction of the conversation went and how the energy changed, I didn't feel her judgement of the other person uplifted them or the group, and this led to a complete change of energy in the mastermind. We need to be very careful of the energy we think about and then express, as otherwise, we may attract more of it. So, get yourself always into a positive mindset, where you can reframe all experiences into learnings, and you will find one good experience will lead to another. Stay in your heart space and come from that place of love when observing others.

6. **Always be very conscious about what you think, say, and do. Make it a habit to seed the subconscious brain with flowers rather than weeds. In other words; positive intention rather than the opposite.** Everything is taken literally by the subconscious brain, so be careful in voicing your fears and double negatives. Put all words and sentences into a positive phrases that create what you want rather than what you don't want. For example, if Billy wasn't feeling well, it wouldn't be wise for him to say that; "he is feeling ill or sick". Instead, the most positive creation that could come out as voiced energy is, "he isn't feeling his usual perfect health self or his usual best self." That way, he is setting the intention that he is usually in perfect health and he will get back there very quickly. Otherwise, if he had a period of regular sickness and then his boss said something like; "he is always sick," then there is a double negative of energetic voiced energy from two people setting the wrong intention for Billy's health, and he might stay that way for even longer. (Note that, I am not using 'you' or 'I' in this description, as I don't want to create anything, here and now,

in the present moment. In fact, "I, Douglas Gordon, am grateful that you, the reader of this book, are in perfect health in this lifetime always, and I am grateful that you are happy, healthy, and wealthy." I said earlier in the book that your word is your wand, we incant in everything we say and the sentences we say can sometimes be the sentences we condemn ourselves and others to, so make sure you are using words to create what you want, rather than what you don't want. Don't use phrases like "I hope this… doesn't happen". Also, be careful about speaking of something dangerous that happened to someone else, in past, in the present moment to a loved one or a friend. What I mean by that is say Billy had a particular ailment and his friend John went home and to his wife and said, "Jane, did you hear that Billy got this ailment? He told me that if you do this…(XYZ) you can get it this ailment". Now, although John is talking about Billy in the past; he is talking to Jane in the present moment; and in that present moment he is possibly incanting through his worded energy, that if Jane does…(XYZ) then she could get that ailment as well and she might have already done that (XYZ) and start to worry. That worry could create it through her thoughts, feelings and emotions. So be aware about gossip and speaking about someone else's negative past. (I don't know this for fact but I have seen examples of this in life).

7. **Get yourself into a state of feeling worthy to receive your goals. Visualize, feel and see yourself in the energy of already having achieved them.** If, for example, you wanted to own a nice Mercedes, get a vision board and put up a photo of the car. Also, put a photo up of the interior of the car, with the steering wheel facing you, so that way you can visualize sitting inside. Even go for a test drive to put yourself in the very thing you want. It is all about putting yourself into the energy of what you want and to have the feeling of

being worthy to receive your goals and successes. This is why a lot of people who win the lottery go bankrupt in a very short space of time; because they don't feel like they have earned the money.

People sometimes don't feel worthy in relationships as well. I remember when I was a teenager, there was a beautiful girl in my school who I really fancied, and I really wanted to date her. She ended up showing interest, but I sabotaged it, as I didn't feel worthy of her. This was linked to a lack of self-love in myself at the time. In terms of relationships, as a whole, it is very important to feel grateful and worthy for being in a relationship and attracting a loving partner. Sometimes, people can be really good-looking and they don't feel it themselves. They may be an amazing person with amazing energy, but they don't know it in themselves, and that can make them not feel worthy of love. In order to receive, you must believe, so get yourself into a state of feeling worthy, feeling successful, feeling loved, and just know it! A good exercise to do is to look at yourself in the mirror, every day, and say, "I am worthy of love, I am worthy of success". Say it three times every day for sixty days and see how you change.

8. **Celebrate the wins or successes in life with passion and in a conscious manner.** In other words, after succeeding in something, don't go out to a bar and drink yourself senseless. Alcohol is one of the most common tools used to celebrate success, but actually, it lowers your energy frequency, especially the next day. People have said to me that alcohol can be a good way to bond, and I have to say I have had some super nights out with friends and clients where we have had a lot of fun and ended up developing a much deeper relationship. The reason this can happen is that when you drink alcohol, it weakens your auric field, your energy field around your body, so that means that some of your energy will dissipate out more easily towards the other person you are with and likewise, their

energy towards you. If you and they are incredibly positive people with great energy, that is fine, especially if you are in an area with lots of other positive people too. However, if there are negative people around you with low frequency energy and the alcohol is affecting your auric field, you may pick up on lower frequency energy, which is not good for you. That is why, in my opinion, you can go to some bars have a few drinks and the next day feel fantastic and in others, you have less drinks and you feel hungover the next day. Perhaps, in the second example, in that particular bar you may have been sitting next to someone who was negative or angry. So, the simple rule of thumb is to celebrate without alcohol and also celebrate with high vibration people. When I was writing this book, I got into the flow and wrote 10,000 words in a very short space of time.

To reward myself, I went to the local spa, had a massage, a swim, and a sauna. While I was there, I started to visualize it being my swimming pool, in my house as one of my goals. Most importantly though, I was conscious that this was a celebration of my success over the last few days. This in turn, shows gratitude to myself and opens me up to receive even more good things to happen in my life. That evening, after the celebration, I found myself writing even more positively because of being in that energy of celebration. Positive thoughts produce positive energy, and get you into a more positive flow state. Some of the most successful people I know have trophy rooms where they have medals, cups, and photos of their past success. Now, in some cases, that can just be pure ego, however, it can also be a way of reminding yourself of past success and in turn, using the energy of the past success, or the energy in that room, to get you into the frequency of that energy in the present moment and recreate the same success of the past in the present or in the future again.

You can use visualization and make this happen yourself, so try it. Sit in a meditative state and just visualize a time when you won a big deal or met your wife or husband and then go back, in your mind, to the day, week, or even month before you won that deal or met your spouse. What were you doing in terms of actions before the event, where were you, what were you thinking about, how were you feeling, what were the potential ingredients that led you to that success? Once you can visualize those actions or feelings, then celebrate that feeling in your heart and replicate the feelings, the thoughts, and the emotions in your body, mind, and energetic field, in this present moment. Quite often, I will say to a coaching client to remember a time when you were really happy, so, for example, it might be the first time you held your child, kissed your partner, or won a race. This way, they can get back into that positive energy and recreate that feeling in their body again to recreate the vibration, in order to attract more positivity into their life. Like attracts like, so putting yourself into the vibrational energy of the thing you want to happen, is very powerful.

All this might sound a bit far-fetched, but there are many examples of where mindset and visualization techniques work. In the 1980s, four groups of Russian nationals were all training for the same Olympic event. These four groups of athletes were considered equally matched in terms of their abilities in going for the same event. It was their training schedules that marked the difference.

Group 1:    100 percent physical exercise training

Group 2:    75 percent physical exercise training and 25 percent visualizing themselves participating in and visualizing themselves winning the event.

Group 3:   50 percent physical exercise training and 50 percent visualizing themselves participating in and visualizing themselves winning the event.

Group 4:   25 percent physical exercise training and 75 percent visualizing themselves participating in and visualizing themselves winning the event.

This was training for a physical event in the Olympics, the question is; which group won?

It was Group 4. Why? Because they had successfully completed the event and won it over and over again in their minds—so many times that they just knew they were going to win. They had that knowing mindset, knowing that they were going to achieve what they were going to achieve before they'd actually done it. Their subconscious had been seeded with the energy of winning, it was a pattern, it was already won.

A similar example to this is Usain Bolt, who was one of the world's best ever sprinters. He was an incredible runner, and he would win every single time because he visualized himself winning, before the race begun. After breaking the 100 meter's world record with a time of 9.58 seconds in 2009, he was quoted by news media as saying, "I just visualized and then executed my plan." This is what most of the top athletes do in all sports and what you can do in life as well. Even myself, when I was playing top level field hockey, I played center forward for my team. Each week, as I drove to the matches, I would visualize the right forward running to the end line and passing the ball diagonally back to me while I would run into the D and visualize myself flicking the ball into the net. I remember one of my best seasons, I scored 32 goals that year, and half of them came from exactly that move. I would always have a positive Mindset that it was going to happen, I would then act in terms of speaking to the right forward before every game, sharing the Knowledge of what I really wanted him to do, and then I would put a massive amount of Energy in place to MAKE it happen… Mindset, Action, Knowledge and Energy all in play.

Focus on getting yourself into an absolute knowing state that you are going to achieve your goals, put your time, energy, focus, and love on what you want, not what you don't want, whether it be in health, wealth, business, or relationships in your life. Then use my success formula to MAKE it happen!

Remember to find your purpose, and align goals to that purpose and create energy around those goals. Then break those goals down into easier baby steps, and collaborate with people who have other skillsets to help you get there. Plus, set a deadline to complete the goals, and stay on track with consistent, inspired action.

I believe we are all here on this planet for a reason, a purpose, a mission; so, find it, connect to it, plan it out, and go out there and make a difference to your life and the life of others too.

Stress, Anxiety…

There are always going to be ups and down along the journey of success. Success doesn't always go in a straight line; so if you can just reframe all the failures into learnings, knowing that each one, will get you one step closer to your goal. It makes life so much easier. This is why conscious awareness of, one, your own self, two, situational awareness of where you are and what you are looking to achieve, three, organizational awareness within a business of all the people and processes, and four, client awareness in terms of what their needs are; all lead to a much better understanding of how to achieve success. Sometimes, though, when our expectations don't meet reality, we can get stressed and anxious. The trick is to find out what the source of this stress is and deal with it, with a win-win attitude.

I once was in a mastermind session trying to help a business owner who was struggling with anxiety. She was an owner of a manufacturing engineering firm. She was working in a very male-dominated environment, and she had developed a persona of being very tough in the way she dealt with people. She had called for the meeting asking for help with her anxiety. She went on to talk about how stressful it was that her suppliers and staff were lying to her about why they were not able to deliver on time or at all. A lot of these staff had worked with her for years. She was complaining about her staff not being able to give her what she wanted, do the work on time, deliver supplies on time, and be truthful with her as well. She went on to blame them for her stress and blame her anxiety on the stress of running this business and how it was affecting her in a negative way. She relayed how sometimes, she would be driving along and suddenly, she would get anxiety out of the blue, from nowhere. Has that ever happen to you?

One of the other members of the group tried to get her to see that it was her subconscious programs that she was playing in her mind that were the cause of her anxiety and that if she could let go of them, through awareness, she would be able to release them. This was definitely part of it. However, I believe another part of it was that this woman had spent her entire career negotiating hard with difficult suppliers, and many others to get her products completed in time. She had to play the role of a very strong, tough woman and not to be messed with. I got the impression she was charming to her customers to get the business but not so charming to her staff. She told me herself that she was a control freak, and didn't trust anyone to do the job for her. She felt she had to micromanage everyone and everything, and was aggressive and rude about her own staff, blaming them for their lack of care about her needs and her timings. She also had gone on about how amazing her products were, how successful she had been, and that her business was the best in her state. Definitely a highly successful woman, but here, she was playing the victim and blaming everyone else, without taking responsibility for her own self and wellbeing. Yes, she was stressed, and yes, she was suffering from anxiety, but when we point the finger at others in terms of blame, there are normally three fingers pointing back at us in our hand as well. When I engaged in conversation with her, I went in with a complete intent of love to try and help her. I wasn't doing it for money, nor for attention, just purely to help and support her.

I started to ask her questions to understand her position as much as possible, rather than making any assumptions whatsoever. Remember in any type of coaching, leadership, management role, sales role, or even with a love partner who is suffering, always seek to ask questions with empathy and compassion to understand where they are and what is going on in their head. Never make assumptions. We all see things in different ways.

Once I had asked a series of questions, it was very obvious to me that this lady because of her control issues and lack of trust in her employees; her staff and her suppliers, in turn, had started to not trust her or respect her. Otherwise, they would be delivering on time for her, trying to add as much value for her as possible. I also realized that she was blaming everyone else and not taking responsibility in the way of a conscious leader. Conscious leaders know that they must lead by example, give trust to gain trust, give a little extra to gain a little extra, and communicate in a kind and empathetic manner for people to really want to go the extra mile for them. During the COVID pandemic when we were all communicating on many video calls, I realized how much people can feel energy, even when you are not in the same room as them, and I truly believe if you continuously think and talk badly about someone, even if they are not in the room, they will energetically feel it. For example, with my energy healing that I do, I have done distance healings on people, sending positive energy to them with conscious intention. At the exact time of doing the healing, I have had feedback from their loved ones telling me that the person got out of their sick bed and felt better. People feel energy, so control your thoughts and take this game of life as a game.

Take it as a challenge to see if you can remain positive and emotionally intelligent even in the tough times and challenges. I am not saying it is always easy, but if we can reframe a negative interaction with someone as a lesson, or a challenge to help you stand in your own inner power and reframe it as an opportunity: to self-regulate yourself, breathe deeply, and ask yourself, "Why has this person or situation come into my life? What is reflecting back here, that I can learn from or grow from? What is this person going through, themselves, to be acting in this way? What have I done in the past few days, weeks, or months that this could be a karmic lesson coming back to me for a reason or something I did? Is there anything I can use in terms of learnings in this interaction to help others and turn my mess into a message and give it meaning?" Hurt people sometimes hurt people, so sometimes, it can be useful to ask empathetic and compassionate questions to check on the other person and see if you can help them to get what they want, rather than pushing your own agenda to try and get what you want. If someone attacks you verbally, instead of retorting, try asking them questions. First, acknowledge their pain and feelings with a statement like, "I understand you are upset with me, and I am sorry if I upset you. I want to do everything possible to help turn this situation around for you." That way, you are first appreciating where they are and acknowledging their feelings of upset. Then, another good question to ask is, "Are you alright? Is there anything else I can do for you to help you feel better? Is there something else that is going on in your life that is stressing you out that I can help you with?" Rather than retorting, this approach can sometimes diffuse the interaction quickly and change the situation to create win-win for both of you. This way, you are creating a collaborative environment to work together to solve their needs, and you are there for them, on-board, ready to support.

 Another useful idea to consider with a loved one, is you that love them and they love you, but we are all human and sometimes stress can cause people to do and say things which do not show their best self.

So, if your loved one suddenly starts to take that stress out on you, and lash out, rather than getting wrapped up in their energy, consciously ground yourself, while imagining a violet funnel of light taking away any negative thoughts around you or anything negative being said to you. Then have conscious awareness that your partner might just be vented to you because you are their nearest and dearest and they trust you. Use the navy seal box breathing technique to breath in for four seconds, hold the breath for four seconds, breath out for four seconds, hold the breath out for four seconds and then do the whole process four times. It calms the central nervous system down and allows you to respond rather than react in a more positive way. Calmly holding space for your loved one, when they lose it, can be a very powerful way for allowing them to calm their own selves down. On top of this, while you are doing the box breathing technique you can press your finger-tips strongly into the palms of your hands and hold hard, for very effective stress relief. It's almost like squeezing a stress ball. Finally, remember, that quite often when we see our loved ones in a state of stress we want to fix it as quickly as possible because we love them. However, sometimes it is best to just listen with love before giving any solutions and ask them, "would you like me to give you solutions to help or for me just to listen". Quite often it is just to listen.

Going back to the lady boss, deep down under the tough mask, I felt she had a soft heart that just wanted to be loved and because she had spent so much of her life being in this tough, masculine energy that she longed to be her true, authentic self, with more of a balance between the masculine and feminine energies. When you are always acting in a way that is a mask and not your true self, your heart self; is it any wonder that your body would go into a state of disharmony? A state of anxiety? When your head and your heart are not aligned in terms of the way you think, talk, and act; then there will be an imbalance within your energy field, and that will cause disharmony, stress, and anxiety. Whether male or female, we all have masculine and feminine energies within us. The masculine energy is more about action and doing, whereas, the feminine energy is more about creativity and connection. I will reiterate it is not that all men are action-orientated and all women are creative— I am just talking about the types of energies, and that they are labeled as divine feminine energy and divine masculine energy. The ideal human would have a perfect balance of both, regardless of being in a male body or female body in this lifetime. In a business sense, then you would be able to come up with a great idea and execute it with precision. So, in summary, connect to your heart self, be your authentic self, don't negatively think or gossip about others and I bet you will have better mental and emotional health, all round.

Going back to the lady boss, I realized she was so wrapped up with the symptoms, rather than the source of her problems. From my questioning and her answers, the true source of the problem was a lack of self-love for herself; and this stemmed from a father-daughter relationship where she craved his love and attention more than he was able to give, as he was busy providing for the family. No fault of hers or his—they were just doing the best they could with the resources and circumstances they had. All the lack of trust came from not loving and trusting herself – how can you trust others if you can't trust yourself. Then the control issues, came from not being able to control how much love and time she got as a child from her dad. Also from my analysis, her complaining and blaming of others came from a head and heart misalignment of the path she was following in life. Sometimes when you follow a path of ego and money rather than a path that makes your heart sing you can feel hurt and unhappy inside as there is no fulfillment within. As they say hurt people sometimes hurt people. Through the Awareness, Acceptance, and Affirmation process I went through earlier, added in with a bit of forgiveness and understanding for her father and herself, she might just be able to let go of those energies and start to feel more love for herself.

Then, by doing so, she will potentially cure the 'source' of her anxiety and emotional stress, leading to a higher vibe energy frequency and in turn attract different people and more positive interactions into her life. I also suspect these 'symptoms' of underperforming staff might just go away.

When we take responsibility for our own selves and we change, it is remarkable how the people and interactions we have, change too. Like attracts like so if you want positivity and love in your life, don't just expect it; give it out first.

# SUCCESS WITHOUT STRESS: MIND, BODY, AND SOUL ENERGY TECHNIQUES

Stress is a normal fact of life. How we view the situation, perceive the situation, and deal with the situation is the differentiating part of whether or not we allow it to affect us. You are the CEO of you and you decide for you. How you react—or even better, respond—to any situation, is entirely up to you and your emotional intelligence. Some people can get slapped in the face and cry about it, others laugh about it. You can let something stress you out, or you can take it as a gamified challenge to see if you can pass the emotional intelligence and mental agility test to be the most conscious human, leader, or partner you can be. Emotional and mental turmoil, or tests, can cause stress in some circumstances, and I truly believe that my morning energy optimization routine will help you elevate your ability to deal with these, as long as you are consistent in your practices.

In my view stress is probably the largest cause of disease and ailments in the world today. Your body is made up of cells that are interconnected through energy. Every cell in your body vibrates at a frequency, and your body also regenerates cells over and over again. Stress is when the resonance of the energy in your brain, your heart, your gut, or any part of your body is not aligned to its natural state of harmony.

In my personal experience, back in 2008, I was having relationship issues with both my wife and my boss at the time. I can easily point the finger at them and say it was their fault, but as we know when you point the finger, you have three fingers pointing back at you as well. Deep down, I was stressed because I wasn't happy in what I was doing in my life. It might have been because I wasn't living my true purpose in life. Or that I didn't have the awareness of being able to link what I was doing in the job to an end person and how it added value to their life in some way or form to give me a sense of meaning in what I was doing. Alternatively, I just didn't feel self-love for myself. There are so many potential causes mentally and emotionally. On the physical side, I was playing top level sport, but then drinking far too much alcohol with clients and friends. I was also eating far too much red meat, sugar, and many others things that do not add value to your body. The stress, anxiety, and worry after 2008 built up so much that I suffered with major digestive issues that led to the need for the two operations by the end of 2009. Then, after the operations didn't go so well, I ended up having chronic pain for the next three years.

So, why am I telling you all this? The reason is, that the mental strain, the emotional ups and downs, and the sabotage in terms of diet on the physical side all affected my body and my mindset in a negative way. It is so important to maintain your body and your energy to the highest level always. Even just on a basic physical level; your body will go through wear and tear at times through playing sport, injuries, or even just aging. When you look at yourself in the context of having a physical, mental, emotional, and spiritual side to you, it gives you an understanding that you need to look after all four of these areas. The mental and emotional side link into improved emotional intelligence and self-love. The spiritual, is more about the energetic side, a sense of growth in life and connection to your inner self. The physical is the easiest place to improve immediately with good nutrition, proper sleep, and exercise.

Sometimes though, in the hard knocks of life, you may get hit physically with an ailment or an injury, and that can also add in stress. I still believe that we sometimes create these physical ailments through bad thoughts, words, and actions. However, sometimes, an energetic field can be disrupted by energy from outside of us, and that energy could lead to a bad decision and an ailment or injury. For example, you might be playing soccer, and during the game, someone hits you, then your ego crops up, and you decide to go in with a hard tackle to get back at them, but it goes wrong, and you get injured. If you were in a heart state, you would forgive and move on, rather than retaliate. I have noticed in my life that people who get bugs like colds, flu, and other similar viruses are more likely to get them if they are in a more negative state. Maybe they are depressed, stressed, angry, or even just really tired and lacking energy. All of these feelings will lower the frequency of your life force and immune system. Then, when you come into contact with someone who has a virus, you are more susceptible to it. Let's face it: the higher your energy, the more energy your immune system will have to keep these bugs away.

Talking of bugs, I went to a conference in 2022 with around 1,000 people there and was shaking hands all day for two days. I was tired from working hard and sleeping too little, and my energy levels were low. I then went out after the conference and drank a few glasses of wine, reducing my energy further. Surprise, surprise, a couple of days later, I came down with a virus and was diagnosed with COVID. Which, in case you are reading this many years after this book was written, COVID is a very contagious flu that put the entire planet into a pandemic where most people had to hide away in their homes for almost two years. When I woke up on the morning I got tested for the virus, I was in a bad state.

I had a migraine like the worst hangover you can imagine, my balance was a bit off, and I was feeling drained of energy. Now, if I was a person to read all the news of all the deaths and hospitalizations of people and was to become fearful of it, that vibration of fear could have brought on anxiety, stress, shortness of breath, and many others things that we can create based on reading certain fearmongering stories and create a worse reaction than was necessary. In fact, in some aboriginal cultures in history, the village where they lived would have a magic man, and this magic man would have the power in a magic stick to kill people if he pointed the stick at you. Now, realistically, it was an absolute load of rubbish, but the people had created the propaganda around the story so much so that the entire culture believed it was the absolute truth. And because of that belief, when he pointed that stick at someone, they died, not because of the magic of the magic stick, but because of the psychological belief of being a victim, and that psyche created the outcome. Your brain is a very powerful tool, so use it wisely and believe in positive miracles, not negativity. Some people get cancer and are told they have four months to live by their doctor, and exactly four months later, they are dead. Other people are told they have four months to live, and they decide that is not the truth, and they change their lives completely to live longer. From my healing experience, I have come across many miracle stories of people completely healing themselves naturally. Anything is possible. It is up to you what you believe and whether you take action to change your thoughts, your habits, and your emotions to change your life, for the better.

I took the diagnosis of COVID as a challenge to see how quickly I could heal myself, a mini goal that made something that was a bad experience into a more fun experience. I gamified the situation. 24 hours later, I walked 2.2 km in a remote area with nobody around. On top of this my headache was gone within less than 12 hours, and I was feeling much better all around.

The first question I asked myself was; *Why did I get it?* Well, as I said, I went to a big conference where I met a few old friends and went back into the 'old Doug' mode of drinking alcohol in celebration of a big event being back on after the pandemic. The alcohol lowered my frequency, and then, I hugged a friend who I consequently found out had COVID already. I also think it was a gift in one way, as it gave me the inspiration to write this part of the book to add value to people. What we need to remember is we can be purposeful, energized, aligned to our goals, but sometimes, life can send us a few tests along the way, just to check to see if we are still committed to our mission and have faith in our own inner power. I personally believe we sometimes also create this drama, ourselves, to test us and push us outside of our comfort zone. Or, on the flip side, sometimes, self-sabotage can kick in when things are going too easy.

The tools I mention below are no substitute for medical advice; they are just things that I have used personally, for many years, when I have had a flu bug, or any virus, in order to help aid in terms of traditional medicine. I will say I didn't take a single drug, not even a paracetamol, and in fact, since 2013, I have taken very little pharmacy drugs at all, no antibiotics, and the only vaccines have been for travel purposes. Hopefully, there will be some alternative tips you may find useful.

Firstly, I had no fear whatsoever. I knew I could heal myself and heal myself quickly and took it as a fun challenge. This is so important in any ailment in life. It does help when you've had a near-death experience and have no fear of death. But having said that, the pain I went through in terms of before the NDE and after the operations I had, were something I am very glad to have had in the past, and to be honest, COVID was easy in comparison.

COVID is a respiratory virus that doesn't like heat, so I did steam inhalation at least twice a day for ten minutes each time, breathing in and out through each nostril and also the mouth with a sense of vigor.

While breathing in the steam, I did the "Wim Hof" breathing exercises, breathing in and out vigorously. Basically 30 deep breaths in and out at a pace. I put orange peel, cinnamon, and sea salt in the boiling water, just to make it more pleasant. It was also great for freshening up the nasal passages. Wim Hof is an amazing guy who uses vigorous breathing techniques to oxidize the body, thus alkalizing the body and in turn, massively improving the immune system. They say it is much harder for the body to get ailments in an alkaline state. Acidity in the body is not good for your health.

I also used a cotton bud to tickle the inside of the nose, to make myself sneeze a number of times. The idea being that I would eject some of the germs as quickly as possible. I have done this in the past when I felt I was getting a cough, and very often, it got rid of it before it started. If you think of physics, if dirt or viral particles go into your lungs, they can potentially cause an infection, so if you can eject them as quickly as possible, before any infection can take place, then you will have a speedier recovery.

I also did regular water enemas using a small 11 ml syringe, with clean bottled water, to bring the bug through quickly and keep the colon and bowels cleansed. I usually squirt three to four syringes of the 11ml up the anus and then push it straight out into the toilet. I have actually been doing this for over 13 years since my operations back in 2009. I do it to ensure soft stools, so that there is no damage to the anal region. Since doing it, I rarely get cuts, piles or hemorrhoids, which I used to all the time. The other reason I do it is to keep the bowel area clean. I found that I was getting residue waste left just inside the bowel, and that was causing itchiness as well, which kept me awake at night, for years, until I started doing the enemas. I also thought about: how, when a baby has a fever and has a swollen throat, the doctor will often prescribe anal suppository paracetamol to help the fever. I realized that if a paracetamol up the bum can cure a headache and make someone feel better, if we flip that perspective, how it is going to work if you have waste stuck in your bowel all the time. Perhaps this is the reason why a lot of men get prostate cancer in the latter years of their lives? Not saying it's definitely the case, but if you had your own hand in a bucket of poop for sixty years, I'd say your hand would not be in the best state due to osmosis after that length of time. So, why not ensure a clean area as well. I also find it saves toilet paper, as the flow is easier, quicker, and smoother. Thus saving the environment in one way as well. In terms of COVID, though, I had heard it sometimes led to a sick and bloated feeling in the stomach. In my experience in the past, enemas help reduce that. Even before my operations in 2009, I spent many years with reflux and a hernia at the top of the stomach, and I realize now it was down to slow bowel movements and having to strain. The straining caused the stomach issues, the enemas allowed easy flow with no straining, and my stomach issues went away. I also realize that the fullness of the bowel and the ability to urinate are interlinked. Quite often, I would have absolutely no feeling of needing to urinate, but then do a water enema, release pressure in the area as I would poop, and then, would find I would urinate for quite some time afterwards. Normally when needing a pee like this I would have felt the need beforehand. Many specialists told me the two were not interlinked, but in my personal experience, that was not the case—the full bowel was pushing on the vessels between the kidneys and the bladder and as soon as the pressure was released through bowel evacuation, suddenly, the pipes flowed all round. This, again, is why I think enemas are brilliant, as they 'may' help with kidney problems, bowel problems, bladder problems, and prostate as well. This is just my viewpoint though; please seek medical advice with a doctor or specialist before basing your prognosis on my own experience. I am just sharing in case it helps someone.

Another thing I did to help the virus was to drink an herbal tea two to three times a day with turmeric, garlic, ginger, cayenne pepper, cinnamon, black pepper, thyme, apple cider vinegar, cloves, lemon, and honey in it. Turmeric is a natural anti-inflammatory, helps digestion, and is apparently good for clearing out bugs. I experimented with it years ago and overdosed on it by mistake and felt dizzy. It is a bit like aspirin, and the Indian culture use it as a natural anti-depressant as well. It absorbs more easily into the body if mixed with black pepper. Garlic is a natural antibiotic. Ginger helps the digestion, and your digestive system uses a massive amount of energy in your body, so easier digestion potentially means more energy for the immune system. Cinnamon regulates the blood sugars in the body. Apple cider vinegar is great for cleaning out the bugs in the digestive tract, and it helps digestion as well.

I also took three drops of oil of oregano (the Athina brand) two to three times a day, which is supposed to be very good for the gut. I drank loads of water with 1,000 mg of Vitamin C + zinc and 1,000 mg of multivitamin and took Vitamin D3 several times a day.

Another tip is to eat food that is either healthy vegetable soup or smoothies, so that it is easy to digest and gets the nutrients into the system without using up too much energy.

I also recommend lots of sleep. I am one of those people who can live on six hours of sleep. Having said that, if you are exercising and working hard, sleep is important.

Blood flow in terms of exercise is great to get the toxins out of the body. It also helps get oxygen around the body and, in turn, makes the body more alkaline, which helps you heal.

I also did an energy healing on myself. The idea of how healing works is to connect to the energy that is all around us and send positive flow and the intention of love and healing to the areas of the body that need it. Pain is a signal indicating the vibrational resonance, in that area of the body, is out of its normal synced vibration. Through my energy healing; I can energetically re-align the vibration back in to the right frequency, and then, in turn, the areas heal or the pain releases.

Another tip is that orgasms help release endorphins into the body, which actually helps get rid of headaches. It's a brilliant technique and a lot of fun as well. And speaking of endorphins, add in a bit of laughter yoga, and the happy factor speeds up the healing too. Laughter yoga is where you make yourself laugh for fun, and then quite often after a while you find yourself laughing at yourself laughing for real. It's great fun and I have done this with many large groups of teams in companies. One time I had over five hundred people laughing out loud at once.

All of these ideas and bio-hacks are tips that worked for me. You can experiment and see what works for you. Having said that, I truly believe that you can let go of any dis-ease in your body or life. It is important to have the awareness of the source or reason that the ailment or dis-ease was energetically created. It might have been bad daily habits, or allowing negative treatment from someone that you didn't deserve, or even choosing to stay in a job or relationship that didn't serve you. All of these can bring bad energy into your field and this is when dis-ease in the body can be created, over a long period of time. The body is telling you that you need to change something, and the ailment is a serious wakeup call that you are on the wrong path or doing the wrong habits. Through awareness, acceptance, and appreciation of everything in our lives, we can change and reframe our mindset, our habits, and the way we feel to allow the dis-ease and dis-harmony within the body to dissipate and go. Unfortunately, though, sometimes, people are taught or encouraged to try to "fight" dis-ease all the time, and I believe fighting anything only creates more disharmony within the body or in their lives. Healing and wellbeing comes through love for oneself and through creating a positive vibration within. With this in mind, I realized that in order to perform to the highest level, I needed to be open to all aspects and ideas of wellbeing, and this is what led me on a path of energy healing. I started to study healing and became a master teacher healer of several modalities of healing. I realize that, when somebody gets an injury on their knee or any area of their body, the vibration of energy in that area is knocked out of alignment, and that mis-alignment sends a signal of pain to the brain to tell you there is something wrong there. I have learned, that it is possible to connect to the universal energy all around us and then channel that high vibrational energy, into ourselves, mixing it with positive vibes, love and intention. Then sending it to the area that needs to be healed. People intuitively knew that in the past, and that is why often, as kids, when we fell over and hurt ourselves our mums or dads would automatically put their hand on the sore bit and tell you it will be fine. Instinctive love from a parent to a child without even thinking about it and a suggestive energetic affirmation, affirming it will be fine. In other words; love and intention to create healing. I have found you don't even need to put your hands on the area to heal it. When you have trained in the healing arts, you can utilize intention, positive vibes, and love to heal anyone, anywhere in the world, as we are all interconnected. Energy has no limits and it can go anywhere. Let's face it: I can speak to you on a phone on the other side of the world, and the energy sounds exactly the same as if you were in the room. I have healed people all over America, in the UK, Ireland, Australia, South Africa, Holland and Belgium from my house in Dublin while they were in their own country at the other end of a zoom call.

I don't believe, I am special. I have just learned how to open up my energetic channel to hardwire into the universal energy all around us and intently send positive energy anywhere I want to. I actually believe anyone can do this, and the higher vibe positive energy you have, the more effective the channel of healing energy you will be able to use. It's a bit like a pint of Guinness; if the pipes are clean in the pub, it tastes better. If you are energetically in the best state, then you will be able to channel more positive energy into others.

Your health is your wealth and high positive energy is key to creating success in life. Energy healing is a great way get you charged up ready for that success. It can also be used for healing injuries and ailments. I have testimonials from a CEO who was told he would never run again, because of his knees, and he ended up running a marathon in his fifties after the healing, he had with me. I had another CEO with a lump on his testicle, and after the healing, it went away. I had an international sportsman who had a knee injury and was told he wouldn't be able to play for four weeks, but after a healing with me he was back playing the next week. I had another older guy who had a back problem, and after the healing, he was able to pick up his grandchild, for the first time. I also have a video testimony from an attorney who had long COVID, and it was gone after the healing. Someone else, had brain fog, and after one healing it went away too. One lady had migraines for months, and they were gone after one session with me. My son, at age 7, had a large splinter in his foot, and we couldn't get it out, my ex-wife wanted to take him to hospital, instead I gave him a healing, and it popped out by itself. Only this weekend, now age 17, he had a muscle strain from overdoing it in the gym, I gave him a ten-minute healing and it was fixed the next day. Another lady kept manifesting bad luck for her life, and I managed to change that, and she started to manifest good things, instead. She also did a video testimony for me, which is on YouTube. One hedge fund manager was suffering from anxiety because he had been in a bomb explosion, and after the healing, he was no longer anxious. Another guy was an alcoholic, and after the healing, he never touched alcohol again. Another lady was attracting bad relationships, dates, or partners into her life and after some healing, mindset coaching and dating advice, she found her soul mate. I also have testimonials from a burn victim who had second-degree burns. Three days later, after the healing, it was much better.

In 2022 was even awarded "International Healer of the Year" by the International Association of Top Professionals, which was announced publicly on the digital board in Times Square. I also was awarded "Global

Man of the Year" in 2022 by *Global Woman Magazine* for contributions to humanity for doing thousands of hours of mental wellness coaching, healing, and business advice for charity to help people during the COVID pandemic. I only say this; to showcase that it actually works, and the feedback, testimonials and votes led to the awards.

If you can get your body into the best possible state, you will perform better, feel better, succeed more, and feel less stressed. Some people come for healings and coaching not because they need it, they just want to maintain optimal health and the highest amount of energy possible.

For me, personally, all of this helped me get back into perfect health and enabled me to perform at the highest level.

# THE SUCCESS FORMULA TO GLEAM YOUR ENERGY OUT TO THE WORLD

I have mentioned my MAKE acronym as a success formula all the way through this book. I truly believe, if you have a positive Mindset, take inspired Action, with good Knowledge of where you are and what you want to succeed in, and have Lots of Vibrant Energy, you can achieve anything in life. I also believe what we go through, we grow through to glow through, and in terms of life. So, I will finish up with another formula with steps to charge yourself up for success. It is another acronym and a formula for increasing your energy, and increasing your sense of love for yourself in a positive way. This formula comes from the word GLEAM.

> G – **Gratitude, Giving, Grounding & Goals.**
> L – **Learning the game of life and to Let go**
> E – **Energy and Emotional Intelligence**
> A – **Authenticity and Affirmations**
> M – **Meditation and Meaning**

So with the GLEAM acronym, I feel we are human beings with energy within us, energy flowing through us, and even energy binding our cells in unison. I believe the true us is not the body we are in, it is the energy within. The word GLEAM refers to light shining from within you, and as we know, light travels super-fast, which means it has high frequency, high vibration, and high energy. So, if you can GLEAM at the highest level, then you will be in the highest state of positive energy, shining your light wherever you go. So, let's take a look at that acronym and how we can implement it into your life…

"G" firstly stands for "Gratitude."

Everyone talks about the attitude of gratitude and how important it is, but why is that? The answer is simple, if you think about it, if you have a child and you give that child a present and he or she isn't grateful for that present, would you feel like giving that child anything else? Of course not, right? So, why would the Universe, God, your own subconscious, or whatever you believe in, give you anything else if you are not grateful for everything you have been given in your life up to now, however small? So, it is paramount that you are grateful for the simplest of things in life; such as your health, your family, your friends, the food on your table, your bed you sleep in, even the testing people that you have learnt from… everything. That way, by being grateful for all you have, you then will open yourself up to feel worthy to receive more. Or if you believe in a higher power, and you show gratitude for all the gifts you have already been given, then the higher power will feel like giving you more.

I believe that life is a gift, a chance to experience life in physicality. I talked about finding your purpose earlier on in the book, but one of our purposes in life is to enjoy all the gifts of living a physical life and that includes being grateful for your five senses. The gift of sight and being able to see the beautiful things in life such as the lakes, the mountains, the sun, the sky, the stars, the faces of loved ones, the smiles, the tears, and even the creations we humans have built. The gift of hearing and being able to hear the rustle of the leaves in the wind, the chirping of the birds, the crashing of the waves on a seaside, the trickle of a stream, and the sound of someone saying that they love you. The gift of touch and being able to feel your partner's hand on your face, a hug, a kiss, holding hands, the wind in your face, the rain in your hair, and even the sun on your skin. Also, the gift of feelings, such as the gift of love in your heart, pleasure, pain, happiness, sadness—without the dark, sometimes, you can't appreciate the light. The gift of taste and being able to taste chocolate, cheese, the juice of an orange, even a cold drink on a hot, sunny day. The gift of smelling a flower, the dew in the morning air, the delicious food we cook, and even the fun of smelling your own farts. These are all gifts that sometimes we can take for granted and do not appreciate in gratitude, however, if you can live in awe of all of these sensations in a mindful manner as the gifts of life, then even the simple and small things can become a pleasure to experience again and again. Be grateful for all of these gifts of life and you will enjoy life so much more.

Gratitude gets your body and energy into a high vibe state, and as said a few times in this book "your vibe attracts your tribe". So, if you get yourself into a state of consistent gratitude you will attract more positive high vibe people and more positive happenings into your life.

The second "G" I mentioned was giving. Giving to others is the greatest gift you can give yourself, and it brings an energy of contentment and love when you give to another human being. We are taught that the more you give, the more you get, and to an extent, that is true, but only if you give without the expectation of receiving anything back, purely giving out of love. Whereas, if you give as a trade, expecting something back, then the Universe or even your own subconscious sees that, and it doesn't work. During the pandemic, I gave over 1,000 hours of my time to help people with mental wellness issues and to help business owners to be successful for free. I did it out of love, and I did it purely to help my fellow humans in need. I never expected anything back. Yet, at the end of every day when brushing my teeth, I was able to look in the mirror and say to myself, "I am a good person, I love you." People talk about self-love and pampering yourself, and I agree with that to an extent, as I love a good massage or a spa day, but when you go out and give to others, and then you look at yourself in the mirror, you will be able to look at yourself in a sense of love and admiration. Sometimes, we also learn ourselves; when we help others, and I learned so much from all the experiences and problems these people were going through. It has allowed me to utilize those learnings to help more people.

The third "G" is Grounding, and what I mean by that is grounding yourself every day, as I mentioned earlier in the book. As I said before, you can walk into a room and feel when two people have had an argument based on the energy, so with Wi-Fi and five billion phones out there, surely there is a possibility that sensitive people who can feel energy, might be distracted by the energy around them. Also, we all are psychic to a degree, and I mentioned earlier that psychic people can pick up on other people's thoughts, so make sure you ground yourself properly by using the techniques I discussed in the chapter on my morning routine, so that you are thinking your thoughts and not being influenced by someone else's.

The final "G" is Goals, and here I will reiterate, what I said in the chapters on goals. Find your true purpose, and then, align goals to that purpose or mission to give you direction in life. Also, have a look at all the areas in your life, such as your financial wellbeing, your career, your love life, your hobbies, your health, your family, and your living environment. Then analyze all of them in a state of awareness, in terms of understanding, where you currently are and where you would like to be, and then, align goals to get there. Remember, if it is a big goal, break it down into baby steps.

The first "L" is Learning from the lessons in life. Let's face it, we all go through hardships in life, and these can come in the forms of relationship breakdowns, ailments, job losses, deaths of loved ones, or many other factors that if not dealt with in an emotionally intelligent way, it can lead to stress, anxiety, and even depression. I went through all of these, and I truly believe that these hardships in life are there for us to learn from, to grow from, to evolve from, in order to become a better version of ourselves and also to utilize and teach other people so they can go through them in an easier fashion. Thus, turning a tragedy into a triumph.

In fact, having had a near-death experience, I truly believe that we come down to this planet to play the game of life to see if we can learn, grow, and evolve to be the best versions of ourselves and even get back into an enlightened state of consciousness. In other words, become the best version of yourself. This means that each time we come here, we test ourselves with these hardships to see if we can get through them and learn from them in a positive fashion, in order to teach others and in turn, raise the overall consciousness of the entire human race. Based on this belief, maybe, if you are one of those people who have gone through a lot of testing times in your life, a lot of hardships in life, maybe stop and pat yourself on the back. Because, just maybe; you have played this game of life so successfully in past lives that this time, you are playing the game of life to a much higher level of difficulty to test yourself to the ultimate, to see if you can still go through all this, grow through all of this, and then turn your mess into a message to give it meaning and help other people. It could be seen a bit like a PlayStation game – you get up to a higher level, each time you reincarnate, to test your skills in this game of life. So, next time you are going through a difficult time, say to yourself, "What can I learn from this situation, or what is mirroring back to me in this situation and what can I utilize in this learning to help others in some way or form?" I also believe we play this game of life as the man, the woman, the king, the queen, the prince, the pauper, the invalid, the Olympian, all to give us different perspectives on life and also to correct or play out karma if need be. Finally, in terms of learnings, I believe if anyone was to take their own life in the way of suicide, they would have to come back and do the same level, story, or game all over again. So, why not just get it done this time around?

Also, learn to let go! When the sun is shining on a flowing river the water gleams, but sometimes, a little bit of the river can get stuck on the side, and it can go stagnant. That is a bit like you. The energy flows through your body beautifully, except when you get stuck emotions within, such as anger, resentment, lack of forgiveness, and guilt. These are all energies of the past. Stop focusing on the problems of the past and let go, so that you can focus on your fabulous future instead. Also, when you have those suppressed or stuck emotions within, you may be more easily triggered in certain circumstances that remind you of the past, when that negative stuck emotion was created. Emotion, is energy in motion. When it is stuck, it can disrupt the field of energy within your body, and it can also lead to you attract other people who similarly have that same kind of stuck emotions within. Learn the lesson, let go of the past, and watch your life improve for the better.

"E" is for energy, and it is understanding that the spiritual, mental, emotional, and physical energies in your body are all interlinked. If you work on one, it will help the others. For example, if you were to get really physically fit, then your heart would be stronger, and you would be able to cope with strong emotions more easily. If you are able to cope with the strong emotions, then it will help with your mental state as well, as you will be more emotionally intelligent. Which moves onto the next "E:" Emotional Intelligence. This is firstly about awareness of knowing the areas that trigger you or the character traits that you need to self- improve on. Through awareness and acceptance, you can implement change and become a better version of yourself. The next part of emotional intelligence is self-regulation in terms of being able to deal with everyone that come into your life in the best possible manner, especially if they are testing in some form. It is all about creating win-win in the interactions of life, and that includes with your own self. Let's face it: you are the person who talks to yourself the most, so you might as well make it positive. It's amazing how so many people talk to themselves in a way they wouldn't even speak to their worst enemy. You are you best friend, so speak to you in the positive way. Seed your subconscious mind with flowers not weeds. Conscious communication is another part of emotional intelligence, and as I have said earlier, your word is your wand, so be very careful to voice what you want, rather than what you don't want. I also said "the sentences we say can be the sentences we condemn ourselves and others to" so have a conscious understanding and flawless mastery of words and voiced energy. Empathy and compassion are also key parts to emotional intelligence, so really try to understand that we all come from different backgrounds in life, and that can mean we all have different perspectives of the same things. Try and put yourself in other people's shoes, so that you can understand where they are coming from. Ask questions to understand, rather than making assumptions about what they are thinking. Also remember you can fifty different people in a theatre listening to a play and have fifty different perspectives, understandings and ways of seeing that play. So always seek to understand how the other person communicates and then communicate to them from their way of thinking and you will find greater success in your relationships. Finally, on the emotional intelligence side of things, motivate or even better, inspire yourself to be the best version of you, and then inspire others around you to be the same. With inspiration you will turn up as your best self in every situation, every day, charged up ready for success.

"A" is firstly for Authenticity. I believe you chose this body, this space suit you live in, for a reason in this lifetime. The best version of you is you, so be you. Don't try and mask your true personality; let it shine through. It is amazing how, when you are truly authentic and honest in what you say, think, and do, you will find that people will sense it and be more willing to collaborate with you, work with you, and even love you. There are many people who fake it till they make it, but there is only so long you can keep up that mask, you will eventually get found out. Better to be you. I knew one guy who bought loads of fake followers on Instagram and loads of people thought he was better than he was and paid for his services. He made millions, but then he told me that he was depressed and miserable. Why? Because his heart and his head were not aligned, he wasn't being truthful, he was cheating the game of life and the energy of deceit was affecting his heart and his soul. You can only win by being authentic.

"A" is also for affirmations. The more positive affirmations you say to yourself, the better. Everyone gets negative thoughts, so seed your subconscious with as many positive affirmations as possible, and you will create neuroplasticity in the brain and create new patterns of more positive thinking. It is like going to the gym; you need to do it every day. As I said above, plant flowers in your brain, rather than weeds. Say to yourself every day, as many times as you can, affirmations like: "I am an amazing person. I am full of love. I am successful at everything I do. I am creating positive relationships with everyone I meet. I am happy, healthy and wealthy always. I am in perfect health. I am gleaming with positive energy every day and that energy is having a positive effect on everyone I meet. I am safe and secure, the universe has my back." The more you hypnotically tell yourself these the more you will create them in your psyche as part of you. See what other positive affirmations you can add and say them as many times as you can, and over time watch the magic that happens in your life.

"M" is firstly for Meditation. Do you know that 85 percent of billionaires, multimillionaires, sports stars, actors, and athletes all meditate? I found the same ratio with the 300 plus radio guests that I have had on my show. The reasons are listed below.
1. Meditation can help you to reduce stress to increase energy for life. It allows you to use breath movements and intentional flow around the body to bring a sense of relaxation and peace. The intentional use of the breath can also help send positive energy and love to those areas that may need it. Focusing on the breath and breathing full breaths intentionally help to bring oxygen and blood flow around the body, which can oxidize the body and create a more alkaline state, which helps the immune system.
2. You can use it as a tool to connect with your inner self and your heart self, to create more positivity in your life. While in a meditative state, I will often affirm, "I am Doug Gordon. I am my heart. Please let me connect with the hearts of everyone I meet in order to bless, rather than impress." What I am doing there is getting myself out of my head space and into my heart space. Ego and fear tend to come from over thinking and being in your head space. Whereas, in your heart space you are in a higher place of love. That way, you can make decisions from a place of love, rather than fear, and also communicate with others from that space as well. Interestingly, when I do this before I get on stage to do a keynote, I tend to speak better in front of a large audience. This is because, I am purely trying to add value from that place of love, so by having no fear, I tend to speak more clearly, because I am not thinking about making a mistake, I am just focusing on the added value. Try the affirmation and see if it works for you.
3. You can also use meditation to visualize your goals, visualize with the end in mind, and visualize the steps in terms of how you plan

to achieve your goals. Or even visualize yourself in perfect health, if that is what you want.
4. Group meditation is very powerful and has been proven to help collective goals and prayers happen in all types of circumstances. It is collective consciousness working together. If only we could all meditate together, at the same time, around the world, visualizing world peace, love, kindness, the earth being healed, anything positive would be so powerful. The power of the mind is amazing, the power of the collective mind is incredible.

The final "M" is for Meaning, and by meaning; I mean create a purpose in life, something you love doing, are gifted with the skills to do, and can add value to people in some way. Or, as I said before, "turn your mess into a message and give it meaning"—in other words, take the hardships or learnings in life and use them to help others in some way. The fulfillment of helping others and seeing positive change in their lives is a wonderful gift to yourself.

Let's face it: when you are 100 years of age, you are not going to look back at your life at how much money you have made or how many houses you might have owned. You are going to look back at the legacy you have left, and that comes down to how many hearts you touch, leaving a legacy of love and positivity on this planet that will energetically ripple on forever. This can come down to the simplest of things such as a kiss you give, a hug you hold, and a kind word you pass on. So, go out there and give as many kisses, as many hugs, and as many kind words as you possibly can, and you will live a life of love.

And if you can find your true purpose, you will love what you do, love the people you work with, love the game of life, and love the people you serve with LOTS OF VIBRANT ENERGY.

And remember, when you optimize your energy, you optimize your performance in life, and when you are fully energized you will "Charge Yourself Up for Success in Life, in Work and in Relationships"

Everything in life is energy. Thoughts are energy; speech is energy. Thoughts lead to speech, speech leads to actions, actions lead to habits, and habits lead to destiny. So, start with a positive thought and end with a positive destiny.

Live, love, and laugh, as they say; Namaste!

# APPENDIX:

## BACKGROUND OF THE AUTHOR

I grew up in a normal family—well, as normal as one might get. Some might say my mother was a witch and my father the most competitive person I had ever come across. My father was an orphan by the age of six. His dad died when he was two, and his mum died when he was six. I can't imagine how tough that must have been for him growing up. My father was stressed at times during his working career, and he retired as early as he could, at 55. He was a bit of a party animal and enjoyed a drink or three on the weekends, and in the early part of my adult life, I was exactly the same. He worked hard and he played hard, and I love him with all of my heart and did everything to emulate and copy him to get his attention. He worked in the finance world, so did I; he played field hockey, so did I; he was highly competitive, so was I; he drank a lot of alcohol, so did I; he was the life and soul of the party, so was I. The problem was, I was following his path, his ways and not my own. I know he loved me with all of his heart, but he had a tough childhood with a lot of emotional strain, and I truly believe some of those childhood trauma issues never truly went away, which happens a lot in people. My mother is a lovely person and has followed a path of spirituality and healing most of her adult life. She is a wonderful person, however, she was a worrier and sometimes holds onto fear too much. She is religious and spiritual in one, and I have to say, I am so grateful for her, as in my early years, she would come into my bedroom at night saying prayers with me while rubbing my forehead. Every night, she would tell me how wonderful I was and how kind I would always be, and I believed her, and her words of positive affirmation stuck in my subconscious. My father is very kind and generous, but his parenting was different, and he believed in competition and pushing me hard to succeed. He had gone from an orphan to a multimillionaire businessman and expected high standards in his sons. If I got 70 percent on an exam, he would ask why didn't I get 80; if I got 80, he would ask why didn't I get 90, and so on. So, I never felt good enough and spent most of my life trying to impress him and get his attention and approval. I also became highly competitive, constantly comparing myself to others, which is something a lot of us do.

This competitive nature came out in sport, as it does with most boys, and at 13, I was the southeast of England 100 meter running champion, despite being one of the smaller athletes in the field. Then, at the age of 17, I was playing for one of the top junior hockey teams in Belgium, and by 18, I was playing first team for one of the top senior teams in the country, which had several Belgian international players in the team. This then led me going to Loughborough, the top university in the U.K. for sport and probably the top in Europe. Again, when I arrived, I played first team. However, with the freedom of living away from home, for the first time, I discovered booze and women, and this didn't mix so well with sport and high performance. At the time, Jason Lee, who was the England Hockey Coach in the 2012 Olympics, took me aside one day and told me I had a choice of chasing girls or playing first team hockey. I choose the women and slipped down to the seconds. I look back at the fun I had, but at the same time, the potential was there to excel in the sport, and I wasn't disciplined enough take it.

Once I had finished university, I went into the investment world, selling mutual and hedge funds to global banks, institutional fund managers, stockbrokers, family offices, and financial advisors. During my 21 years in the industry, I went from customer service, to sales support, to sales, to sales manager, to sales director, to head of sales and marketing. During my time in the industry, I worked for some of the largest institutions in the world, which included Fidelity Investments, Lazard Asset Management, HSBC Asset Management, Aviva Investors, Columbia Threadneedle Investments, and Davy Asset Management. I was recognized in the trade press and the national press for success in the city and managed to grow asset management sales for one company from $50 million per annum sales in 2006 to $1.75 billion per annum sales in 2012, and that was just my personal tally. This industry was a lot of fun with clients being wined and dined, lots of golf, watching sport, and many other fun forms of client entertainment. My upbringing in a party environment served me well, as did my communication skills, which I had picked up through chasing women and trying to convince them to go out with me. I loved people and loved my job, but a lot of it was just competition, ego, and money.

I ate at the best restaurants, stayed in the best hotels, rode a number of times in helicopters, limos, and private jets, but despite all of this, I wasn't truly happy within; I didn't truly love myself. I just wanted to be a big man to impress my friends and my father. The thing I loved most about my job was the connections and friendships I made with so many wonderful clients and peers across the industry. I was and still am very good at connecting with people at a heart level and creating long-term, meaningful relationships, rather than just seeing them as clients or colleagues. It was a great life, but the alcohol, the partying, and the bad diet all took their toll, and this badly affected my digestive system.

Outside of work, I was with my first wife for fifteen years. We had our ups and downs, but we loved each other and have two truly wonderful children together. There was emotional baggage; that I felt I was carrying from childhood, and although we had a good relationship, both of us probably partied too much. Our kids are absolutely wonderful humans in every way and I love them with all of my heart and soul. Being a parent is a big learning experience for anyone and not always easy and I am still learning. I believe children, are your greatest teachers, because they reflect back the areas you need to improve on. Our kids made us change for the better in so many ways. One of those ways, was a realization that love was more important than money for me. This made me see my job just as transactional, and I wanted more meaning and more purpose, and love for what I did. I became unhappy and didn't love myself. This lack of love affected the marriage. I wish I had the knowledge I have now as I would have reframed the understanding of my job as helping those Granny and Grandpas retire younger, give more to their children and have a better retirement. I just didn't see it that way at the time and stress came in to play as I wasn't happy in myself.

In September 2008, the stock market and housing market crashed. Despite being the top performer in the U.K., I still got very worried and stressed. We, as a company, had to lay off a number of people, and being very sensitive to energy, I could feel the energy in the company and even the whole of London. It was a very stressful time for everyone, and for me, stress really kicked in. I ended up getting ailment after ailment, seeing doctor after doctor, specialist after specialist, and then, by the end of 2009, I had two operations that went wrong. This led to chronic pain in my abdomen, and sometimes, I would wake up ten times in the night. It took its toll on me, on my marriage, and on my life. Despite this, I managed to continue to perform in my job, and by 2012, I was having great success, even though I was suffering from stress. I had neck pain, back pain, digestive issues, and many other stress-related ailments.

I regularly suffered from a massive build-up of gas in the stomach from stress, which would push up onto the diaphragm, to the extent that it would be hard to breath. This caused major anxiety, to the point where I would get very anxious getting off the train at times, having to walk over London Bridge. Then, in September 2012, I got the norovirus, which is like a stomach bomb, and this led to a near-death experience, which I have detailed in the main body of the book. Even after the near-death experience, my ego still stopped me from making changes in my life, until I had a surreal experience where I was literally touched and marked by what I would call God or universal energy. I had an accident that led to me falling over and cutting my hands and knee to the point where I had two infinity signs in cuts on either side of the letter of the cross INRI on my right hand. This gave me the kick I needed to start the process of changing my life. Again, this is detailed in the main body of the book.

This led me to completely changing my life, becoming a healer to heal myself, then a life coach, business coach, performance coach, then international speaker and radio presenter. It led me on a path of purpose supporting business leaders, sports stars, movie stars, and many others with lots of different aspects of their lives and their businesses. People ask what I do, and I used to say I have a business side and a Buddha side. Stephen Covey, the New York Times bestselling author who sold over two million copies of his book on "Trust" said it correctly when he met me, "Sure you are the energy man, Doug." He was right, everything I do is around energy: whether it be teaching people how to create and deliver a presentation on stage using their voiced energy. Or coaching leaders to use energy to create positivity and connection within their business. Or helping people to increase their energy in order to perform better in work , sport or even relationships. Or training sales teams to increase their positive energy and energy connection with their clients to create more sales. Or to help people to improve their energy to attract their soul mate. Or using thought energy to reframe a situation in someone's mind in order to release energies in motion – emotions, that do not serve them. Or using energy to heal someone of an injury, an ailment or an unwanted mindset.

Positive energy in the body and mind is so important for achieving high performance. Negative stress, though, is an awful thing, and I wouldn't wish what I went through on anyone. What I realize now, though, is I can blame bullying bosses, I can blame my marriage breakdown, I can blame so many external things, yes, but actually, it was how I perceived and reacted to these external factors that caused the stress. As one of my favorite authors, Wayne Dyer, once said, "If you change your thoughts, you can change your life". Now having worked on my emotional intelligence, my self-love, and learning mindfulness, I deal with these stresses so much more easily. I have gone through a lot of crap and am so grateful to have learned from it, grown from it, and evolved into a better version of myself.

It took me almost forty years to realize I love people, I love business, I love sales, I love connecting with people, I love supporting people, I love helping people, I love being on stage, I love seeing good people change their lives, and I love seeing a happy outcome in people's lives. I could have stayed in the investment world with the wisdom I have now, but I need to go on this journey to be able to approach what I do with a mission based around love, rather than ego and competition, because when you do something you love, it is difficult to get stressed doing it, because it just seems like fun. That way I can "Charge myself up for Success" every day.

# ABOUT DOUG D GORDON

Doug is a five times award winning speaker, coach, consultant, trainer and now author. He Global Goodwill Ambassador for Dublin, Ireland, which was awarded by a U.S. Senator for his inspirational work giving back to the community where he did talks and mindset training and then gave all the money to charity. He was also awarded "Global Man of the Year" by Global Woman Magazine in 2022 for his contribution to humanity in terms of doing thousands of hours of mental wellness work and business advice to help people during the pandemic for free. He was also awarded Top International CEO and Top International Healer with the International Association of Top Professionals in 2022.

He is also a radio presenter of a show called Inspirational People, Inspirational Stories which again, he does to give back to others. He has had a mix of New York Times bestselling author, TV celebs, sports stars, famous CEOs, and many other heroic people.

Previously, Doug spent 21 years in the investment world as an investment sales head for some of the largest fund managers in the world, including Fidelity Investments, Lazard Asset Management, HSBC Asset Management, Aviva Investors, Columbia Threadneedle Investments, and Davy Asset Management. He was recognized in the national press

(The Irish Independent and The Irish Times) and was described as "City Heavy Hitter" for the success he had in the industry. He has also been in trade newspapers, such as Investment Week, IFA Magazine, and many others.

Irish Independent newspaper article: https://m.independent.ie/business/irish/davy-appoints-three-city-heavy- hitters-31506422.html

In 2008, when markets fell, Doug suffered from stress. At the end of 2009, he had two surgical operations that went wrong. After three years of chronic pain, he got the norovirus, was rushed to the hospital, and had a near-death experience. Since then, he has become a master teacher healer of Reiki, Seichem, Bio Energy healing, Magnified healing, and Quantum healing.

Article from press about near-death experience: *https://www.investmentweek.co.uk/investment-week/news/3028010/ near-death-experience-prompts-exit-of-davy-am-distribution-head*

He has coached and consulted with Hollywood stars, New York Times bestselling authors, large corporations like Dell, Odey Asset Management, Davy, Ocuco, Sensys, Killeen Engineering, and many more. He has advised government officials on policies such as diversity and inclusion and on mental wellbeing and wellness practices in America, the U.K., Ireland, and Europe.

He also played hockey at national league top division level in the

U.K. and Belgium, captaining and coaching international level players.

Some examples of past keynote speaking events:

Doug has spoken as keynote speaker on the topics of Leadership, Coaching Skills, Communication skills, Sales Skills, Presentation Skills, High Performance Success without Stress, Startup to Scaleup, Emotional Intelligence of leaders, Workplace Wellbeing, Energy Optimization and Conscious living. He has spoken at events such as: the Institute of Directors

Global Convention, Stanford Business School Alumni Conference, One Africa Forum, National Finance Summit, London Investment Summit, National Workplace Wellbeing Summit, All Ireland Business Summit, FIT CEO Conference, InterNations Conference, International Transfer Agency Summit, Association of Key Account Managers Summit, Thrive Festival, Irish BizEXPO, Hyper Sales Growth Conference, Global Woman's Magazine Summit, Performance Optimisation Conference, Dublin Junior Chamberof Commerce, Galway Junior Chamber of Commerce, Tanzanian Chamber of Commerce, National Health Summit, Techconnect Summit, Global Emotional Intelligence Summit, Speak & Write to Make Millions Conference, Good Summit, Business Markets Summit, Dublin Wellbeing Conference, and in many corporations all around the world. I have had the honor of sharing the stage with New York Times bestselling authors, film stars, TV celebs, sports stars, multi-millionaire business owners, and ex- Prime Ministers, just to name a few. He is also a TEDx speaker.

Onstage photo reel on Instagram: *https://www.instagram. com/s/ aGlnaGxpZ2h0OjE3OTE5NTc4OTY2MjA0ODA5?igshid= YmMyMTA2M2Y=*

Below are a few testimonies and links to showcase past feedback...
    70 plus testimonials / recommendations from past clients on LinkedIn: *https://www.linkedin.com/in/doug-gordon-216091b/*

Here are some video testimonials on my work:
    Kapil Khanna, co-founder of the All-Ireland Business Summit: *https://m.youtube.com/watch?v=L02WLT8FVog&feature=youtu.be*

    Suzanne Selvester, TV presenter and bestselling author: *https://www.youtube.com/watch?v=CqMEn3D36b8*

Nina Aouilk, bestselling author and TEDx speaker:
*https://m.youtube.com/shorts/s4v6_xUIRCw*

Marc Hayford, International Bestselling author and speaker:
*https://www.youtube.com/shorts/CnRCZdWtIvQ*

Pat Slattery, International Speaker:
*https://www.youtube.com/watch?v=uqEzg_oFE8s*

2019 D&S SHOWREEL:
*https://youtu.be/3ipIWg4MBpc*

Here is a Twitter feed on feedback on one of my gigs:
*https://twitter.com/_ocuco/status/1009785300632133633*

Other testimonials:

*https://www.instagram.com/p/CU8cC9Nl9t2/?hl=en*
*https://www.instagram.com/p/CHWibfhHms7/?hl=en*
*https://www.instagram.com/p/CGcoX63HVg3/?hl=en*
*https://www.instagram.com/p/CfEVeSklCYz/?hl=en*
*https://www.instagram.com/p/CVxbsxuFIJp/?hl=en*
*https://www.instagram.com/p/CeqhHx8sdA_/?hl=en*
*https://www.instagram.com/p/CbtP5MuKTrC/?hl=en*

YouTube testimonials

*https://m.youtube.com/shorts/CnRCZdWtIvQ*
*https://m.youtube.com/shorts/s4v6_xUIRCw*
*https://m.youtube.com/watch?v=CqMEn3D36b8*
*https://m.youtube.com/watch?v=FTJyHTgZZvQ*

Printed in Great Britain
by Amazon